A Study Companion to
The Bible: An Introduction

Anthony Le Donne

Fortress Press

Minneapolis

D1361340

A STUDY COMPANION TO THE BIBLE: AN INTRODUCTION
Second Edition

Cover image © blueenaylm/iStock/Thinkstock
Cover design: Erica Rieck
Book design: PerfecType, Nashville, TN

Library of Congress Cataloging-in-Publication Data
Print ISBN: 978-1-4514-8362-8
eBook ISBN: 978-1-4514-8424-3

The paper used in this publication meets the minimum requirements of American National Standard for Information Sciences — Permanence of Paper for Printed Library Materials, ANSI Z329.48-1984.

Manufactured in the U.S.A.

CONTENTS

How to Use This Study Companion   v

Introduction   1

1. The Bible: A Gradually Emerging Collection   5

2. From Then to Now: The Transmission of the Bible   13

3. Inspiration: The Claim That God Speaks in a Text   21

4. The Pentateuch, Part 1: Genesis   27

5. The Pentateuch, Part 2: Exodus through Deuteronomy   35

6. The Israelites Tell Their Story: Interpretations of National Disasters   41

7. "Thus Says the Lord": Israel's Prophetic Tradition   51

8. An Alternative Worldview: Israel's Wisdom Literature and Esther   61

9. Israel's Response to God: The Psalms and the Song of Solomon   71

10. Between the Testaments: From Alexander the Great to the Time of Jesus   79

11. The Gospels: Their Composition and Nature   87

12. Four Views of One Jesus: Mark, Matthew, Luke, and John   95

13. The Story Continues: The Acts of the Apostles   103

14. The Pauline Letters: Apostolic Advice to Early Churches   115

15. The Disputed Pauline Letters: Continuing Advice in Paul's Name   123

16. Hebrews and the General Epistles: Messages for Broader Audiences   129

17. Revelation: John's Apocalyptic Vision   137

A Short Guide to Writing Exegetical Research Papers   145

HOW TO USE THIS STUDY COMPANION

In order to read the Bible with understanding, a book like *The Bible: An Introduction* (by Dr. Jerry L. Sumney) can serve as a thoughtful guide. My study companion (the book in your hands now) is designed to enhance your Bible study alongside Sumney's introduction. My hope is that this book will further your understanding of each of the books discussed by Dr. Sumney and to spark your critical thinking about the ancient world in which the Bible was composed. The guide is organized like the textbook. Each part (here referred to as "section" or "chapter") of the guide corresponds to a section in the textbook and typically includes a section summary, key terms with definitions, and questions for discussion or reflection.

Before you begin reading a section of the textbook, or after reading it to ensure you understood the main ideas, read the Sumney Summary. It offers a basic overview of the section's major themes and issues. Before you read a chapter, it might be useful to note the *Key Terms* and *Key Themes*. These are selected lists of concepts particular to a book of the Bible or group of books with the Bible, names of important episodes, or concepts and their definitions. You will want to be at least familiar with these concepts and terms by the time you have finished reading the section.

On occasion I will include a *Primary Text* passage with some discussion of that source. These excerpts from the Bible or other ancient texts are intended to provide additional context and insight for understanding a biblical topic. After you read a section in the textbook, these materials can help further your understanding of the topic or act as touchstones for class discussion or essays.

Immediately after you have read a chapter in the book, you might wish to go through the related *Questions for Group Discussion* and *Questions for Reflection*. You can use these questions to test your knowledge of the basic concepts explored in Sumney's textbook. Some of the questions are intended to focus on reading comprehension. Other questions encourage you to engage in class discussion. In asking these questions as you read, consider whether one of these might serve as a research paper topic.

Finally, this study companion also includes a guide to writing a research paper and a check list for completion. You may use this (in consultation with your professor) to determine an essay topic, monitor your progress, and check your work before you hand in your essay.

INTRODUCTION

A student of English literature who does not know the Bible does not understand a good deal of what is going on in what (s)he reads: the most conscientious student will be continually misconstruing the implications, even the meaning.

—Northrop Frye

Literary scholar Northrop Frye was not a religious man. But because he was an expert in literature, he knew that the Bible was the single most influential library in western culture. He was disappointed by his students at Harvard University and the University of Toronto for their lack of biblical education. While these students were otherwise bright, Frye was unable to discuss the works of English greats like Shakespeare and Blake without also schooling them in what he called "The Great Code." In other words, you cannot unlock poets like William Blake without a reservoir of prior biblical knowledge.

For many religious folk, the Bible is sacred and holy. It communicates the very words of God Almighty. But aside from matters of religion, every person from every walk of life must know something about the Bible to be culturally relevant. Without an understanding of the Bible, the average person will misunderstand key aspects of Jesus, Mohammed, St. Francis, Michelangelo, Galileo, Dante, Spinoza, Blake, Milton, Shakespeare, Bach, Whitman, Lincoln, Darwin, Malcolm X, Tolkien, Bob Dylan, Stan Lee, Stephen Spielberg, Quentin Tarantino, Kanye West, and J. J. Abrams. This list could go on indefinitely. Add also the numerous ways in which the Bible influences politics, geography, and history. In short, a better understanding the Bible will help westerners better understand their culture, their world, and themselves.

So then, where to begin?

Let's begin with a very basic definition: the Bible is a collection of ancient texts authored over the course of centuries. These ancient poems, stories, histories, myths, letters, and visions are from times and places quite different from our own. So not only is the Bible a library of books all wrapped into one volume, but these books vary in "genre." Everyone with a Netflix queue has seen the word *genre*. It is a French loanword that means "kind" or "type."

Question: What kinds of film do you like best?

Answer: I like Science Fiction, but I also enjoy dark comedies.

This is a question of genre. Genres of film include drama, comedy, action, horror, etc. The same goes for books. In the case of the Bible, we are dealing with several overlapping genres. These include:

Poetry—this can be found in Genesis, Psalms, Job, Ecclesiastes, Isaiah, Malachi, Luke, etc.

Narrative—this can be found in Genesis, Exodus, Numbers, Judges, 1 Kings, Jonah, Daniel, Matthew, Mark, Acts, etc.

Legal Instruction—this can be found in Exodus, Leviticus, Numbers, Deuteronomy, etc.

Prophecy—this is can found in Genesis, Numbers, Isaiah, Ezekiel, Jonah, Daniel, Malachi, Matthew, Mark, Revelation, etc.

Apocalyptic—this can be found in Ezekiel, Daniel, Mark, 2 Peter, Revelation, etc.

Aphorism—this can be found in Proverbs, Matthew, Mark, Luke, etc.

Genealogy—this can be found in Genesis, Numbers, Matthew, Luke, etc.

Letter—this can be found in Romans, Hebrews, 1 Peter, Revelation, etc.

Parable—this is quite a difficult genre to define, but it is most obvious in Matthew, Mark, and Luke.

As these examples show, very few biblical books are confined to only one genre. Isaiah is primarily prophetic, but is written in verse in the style of poetry. Jonah is narrative, but shifts to poetry in the middle and then back to narrative. All the while, Jonah has been traditionally thought of as a "minor prophet." Job is a long poem that tells a story, but the poem is bookended by narrative. Luke is largely a narrative that incorporates short sayings of Jesus (also called aphorisms), but Luke also contains hymns (poetry) and a genealogy. Half of Daniel is narrative and half is apocalyptic/prophecy. The Book of Revelation is apocalyptic/prophecy but also includes short letters.

So biblical genres are numerous and complex. Most folks divide the Bible into the following categories: Old Testament (Law, Prophets, and the other Writings), and New Testament (Gospels and Acts, Letters, and Revelation). While these categories are generally helpful, it is better to recognize the varying genres within these larger sections.

Most of the time, genre is simply implied. If I begin with "Once upon a time . . ." it is implied that what follows will be a fairytale. If I begin with "Today the Associated Press reports . . ." it is implied that what follows is news. If I begin with "So a priest, a rabbi, and a penguin walk into a bar . . ." it is implied that what follows is a joke. Likewise, biblical poems don't announce themselves by saying, "This is a poem!" They simply begin. The poets of the Bible simply assume that their audiences know how poems work. When Malachi launched his prophetic argument, he assumed that his audience would know how prophecies work. The first step in understanding the Bible is recognizing how different genres function.

In addition to recognizing genre, it is also important to learn how each genre functioned within the various cultures that produced the Bible. It will be important to know a few things about the historical backdrop of the biblical authors. It will often be helpful to explore the peculiarities of the "original" languages. After all, the Bible was composed in Hebrew, Aramaic (not to be confused with Arabic), and Greek. These languages very rarely allow for a literal word-for-word translation.

My hope is that this guide will unlock a few of these literary and cultural keys as you begin to study the Bible. I trust that in unlocking the sacred texts of the Bible, you will acquire better keys to unlock the many cultural and artistic expressions that require a biblical education. I will go a step further: very few people who read the Bible seriously remain unchanged. Do not be surprised if Bible study leads to personal development. Perhaps you too will learn why so many people have considered the Bible sacred and life-giving.

1

The Bible: A Gradually Emerging Collection

Summary and Learning Objectives

1. The Bible is a collection of writings that vary in authorship, perspective, genre, and date. The Bible represents many ancient voices, so how do these voices differ? After reading this chapter (alongside chapter 1 of Sumney's text), the reader should be able *to identify several such differences.*
2. Groups are formed by commonalities and by identifying boundaries. Many religious groups use the Bible as a boundary marker. After reading this chapter (alongside chapter 1 of Sumney's text), the reader should be able *to talk about why the Bible is used to include and exclude people.*
3. Different groups use different forms of the Bible. After reading this chapter (alongside chapter 1 of Sumney's text), the reader should be able *to identify at least three different collections (or "canons") of biblical books.*
4. Not only is the Bible a library of several books; these books were brought together in a process of "canonization." After reading this chapter (alongside chapter 1 of Sumney's text), the reader should be able *to say why certain books were included in the Bible while other books were not.*

Key Terms

Apostle   Most generally it means one who is sent. In the early church it comes to designate those who are recognized as the authorities in the church, particularly the Twelve (after they replace Judas), James, the brother of Jesus who becomes the leader of the Jerusalem church, and Paul. Others could be apostles in the sense that they were sent on missions by their churches, but these fourteen people were seen as sent by Christ and so as authoritative.

Apostolicity   The virtue having been written by, or related to, an apostle (related to whether books were included in the Bible).

Canon   A group of authoritative writings.

Dead Sea Scrolls   The manuscripts found in the caves around the Qumran compound at the northwestern end of the Dead Sea. Among the scrolls were numerous commentaries on biblical books. These scrolls provide some of the earliest evidence for the form of the text of the Hebrew Bible.

Tanakh   A common name for the Hebrew Bible within the Jewish community. It is an acronym based on the three parts of those texts: the Torah (T); the Nevi'im (N), or Prophets; and the Ketuvim (K), or Writings.

Key Themes

- ▶ the many voices within the Bible
- ▶ the multiple interpretations and uses of the Bible
- ▶ how the Bible was formed
- ▶ the different shapes that the Bible takes

Primary Text

One Book, Many Voices

Many western people, people of faith and otherwise, think of the Bible like a singular textbook. Indeed, the very title "Bible" comes from the Greek word *biblos* meaning "book"—just one book. Yet any person who spends time reading the Bible realizes quite quickly that multiple hands were at work preparing the many different books (most Protestant Bibles have 66 books) that come together to form the Bible. This fact ought to reveal two things about the Bible:

1. For as long as there has been a Bible, people have recognized the value of placing different perspectives together. Some of the books put forth legal instructions for ancient Israelites; others communicate the elegance and loveliness of the path of wisdom. Some of the books contain stories that are family-appropriate; others are decidedly R-rated. Some these book feature a divine voice from Heaven, portraying God as a character in the story; others do not feature the voice of God at all. Reading the various books of the Bible is a process of balancing various perspectives. We are very rarely given a singular view on topics related to God, humanity, and the way the world works. It is also important to keep in mind that not all of these perspectives are harmonious. The New Testament includes the voices of both Peter and Paul, two leaders who are at odds: Paul says of Peter: "I opposed him to his face, because he stood condemned!" (Galatians 2:11). Good students of the Bible must learn to appreciate the tension created by multiple points of view.

2. Traditionally, Western people have held these various perspectives together. The people who composed, edited, and collected the books of the Bible must have been comfortable putting two creation accounts together: compare Genesis chapters 1 and 2. They must have comfortable setting two accounts of the same history side by side: compare the books of Kings and Chronicles. Indeed the first Christians thought it was necessary to include *four different* perspectives on the life of Jesus: compare Matthew, Mark, Luke, and John. With this in mind, we shouldn't expect that the Bible will provide a simple and straightforward answer to any particular question that we might have. The Bible has been used for millennia as a sacred and holy guide. Such guidance

is best heard as a chorus of voices, not a monologue from on high.

It should seem obvious then that no single reader of the Bible will come away with a perfect point of view. I don't doubt that Dr. Sumney and I will differ at times on how to best interpret a passage. I also don't doubt that our interpretations will differ at times from many other pastors and professors who teach about the Bible. There ought to be room enough for multiple voices at the table. Inevitably some voices will be more compelling than others, but multiple perspectives should be seen as a virtue not a hindrance.

In my experience, the students who have the greatest difficulty understanding the Bible are those who seek simple and definitive answers from the Bible. Such readers often resort to just reading a few familiar passages within the Bible. Perhaps the best way to misunderstand the Bible is to neglect the parts that are confusing or troubling. Another obstacle to understanding is this notion: *if my pastor or favorite teacher taught me X, surely the Bible cannot teach something that contradicts X!* I often tell my students to sit down and read a biblical story as if they knew nothing previous about the characters in the story. Sometimes reading a passage with an open mind can reveal something entirely new and bring the text to life in a powerful way.

I also advise my students to *keep reading*! The Bible can be deceptively familiar. For example, almost every child in Western culture has heard the story of Noah's ark. But reading Genesis 6 for the first time as an adult can been a dramatically different experience. Take a look at Genesis 6:1-4. My bet is that the picture book at your grandmother's house doesn't tell of the "sons of God" who have sex with human women and give birth to semi-divine creatures. Or consider Genesis 7:1-3. Did Noah take the animals "two by two" onto the ark, or was it is sets of seven? If you skip passages in the Bible because you think that you already know them, you might be missing out on a fascinating experience. Finally, it is always best to read the Bible *itself* when learning about the Bible. My hope is that you'll keep a Bible handy when you use this study companion. As you begin studying the Bible, I would advise you to be prepared to listen to many voices, not to expect any simple answer to any question that might arise, and do your best to read as much of the Bible as you can.

A Canon of Voices

When did the various books of the Bible become unified? Who decided which books were holy enough to make it into the Bible? What process was in place to ensure the integrity of this unifying effort? These are all questions about the "canon" of the Bible. When used in biblical studies, the term canon means "a group of authoritative writings." However, you may have also heard the term used of official church leaders.

The idea of being "official" is important here. For example, Genesis is *officially* in the Bible. It is included in the Jewish canon, called the Tanakh (Christians think of the Jewish canon as the Old Testament). Genesis is also *officially* in the various Christian canons. The Orthodox, Catholic, and Protestant Churches all hold Genesis as *officially* inspired by God. Whereas a book like the Gospel of Thomas is not in any official canon. This is to say that Thomas is studied by scholars but not held as authoritative by any surviving worshipping community. When scholars refer to the "canonical Gospels" they mean specifically the first four books of the New Testament: Matthew, Mark, Luke, and John. Although we know that Christians were reading the Gospel of Thomas as early as the second century C.E., it was never regarded as officially a part of the New Testament, and in the fourth century it was specifically rejected as unfit for the canon.

It is often difficult to say exactly why one book was included in the canon while another book (which seems very similar in many ways) was excluded. However, we do hear voices from early Christianity that discuss this issue. For example, one of the key virtues of the four canonical Gospels is that they're all connected in some way to an important follower (or apostle) of Jesus. Writing about one hundred years after Jesus, Justin Martyr calls the Gospels "the memoirs which, as I have said, were drawn up by the apostles and their followers" (*Dial.* 103.8). This is interesting because two of the canonical Gospels, Mark and Luke, were not composed by "apostles" of Jesus. Indeed, we have only guesses about the identity of these authors. Mark seems to have been traditionally connected to the apostle Peter. A Christian writer named Eusebius (writing in the fourth century) refers to a connection between Mark and Peter:

> Mark having become the interpreter of Peter, wrote down accurately whatsoever he remembered. It was not, however, in exact order that he related the sayings or deeds of Christ. For he neither heard the Lord nor accompanied Him. But afterwards, as I said, he accompanied Peter, who accommodated his instructions to the necessities [of his hearers], but with no intention of giving a regular narrative of the Lord's sayings. Wherefore Mark made no mistake in thus writing some things as he remembered them. For of one thing he took especial care, not to omit anything he had heard, and not to put anything fictitious into the statements. [This is what is

related by Papias (an early-second-century church leader from Turkey) regarding Mark.] (*Hist. Eccl.* 3.39.15-16).

So while Mark was not written by an apostle, it at least is connected with the memories of an apostle. *So what about Luke?* Traditionally, "Luke" has been associated with one of the apostle Paul's traveling companions by the same name. The Book of Acts is believed to be written by the same author. The Book of Revelation also enjoys a claim to "apostolicity," in that it is connected with "John." It is sometimes called "John's Apocalypse." So we might say that a strong claim to "apostolicity" (or having a strong connection to an official apostle) was an important factor for canonization. Many letters with the apostle Paul's name attached to them are therefore included. The letter to the Hebrews is a notable exception, as it is anonymously authored. However, multiple early Christian sources guess that Hebrews was written by Paul anyway. The modern scholarly consensus is that Paul was not the author.

The key assumption here is that the apostles (those sent out to preach by Jesus) can be trusted to convey divine truth. In speaking of the way the truth was communicated to the church, Clement of Rome says, "The apostles have preached the Gospel to us from the Lord Jesus Christ; Jesus Christ [has done so] from God. Christ therefore was sent forth by God, and the apostles by Christ. Both these appointments, then, were made in an orderly way, according to the will of God. Having therefore received their orders, and being fully assured by the resurrection of our Lord Jesus Christ, and established in the word of God" (First Epistle to the Corinthians 43, written 95–100 C.E.).

Irenaeus, in his work entitled *Against Heresies* (written sometime around 182–188 C.E.), wrote:

Since therefore we have such proofs, it is not necessary to seek the truth among others which it is easy to obtain from the Church; since the apostles, like a rich man [depositing his money] in a bank, lodged in her hands most copiously all things pertaining to the truth: so that every man, whosoever will, can draw from her the water of life" (3.4.1).

Since, therefore, the tradition from the apostles does thus exist in the Church, and is permanent among us, let us revert to the Scriptural proof furnished by those apostles who did also write the Gospel, in which they recorded the doctrine regarding God, pointing out that our Lord Jesus Christ is the truth, and that no lie is in Him (3.5.1).

A similar logic was applied to the Pentateuch (the first five books of the Bible). Jewish tradition held that the Pentateuch was written by Moses. Because Moses received his instruction from God on Mount Sinai (indeed, by God's own hand!—see Exod. 31:18), Genesis, Exodus, Leviticus, Numbers, and Deuteronomy enjoyed a special status within the Jewish canon. So the "five books of Moses" (as they are sometimes called) were the most securely official.

Many of the psalms, short stories, and poems called simply the "Writings" (including Psalms, Job, Proverbs, Ruth, Song of Songs, Ecclesiastes, Lamentations, Esther, Daniel, Ezra-Nehemiah, 1 and 2 Chronicles) were among the least secure. Indeed, during the time of Jesus, it is quite possible that the "Writings" were not yet officially part of a recognized canon of Scripture. Among the fragments of the Dead Sea Scrolls (an ancient Jewish library found in Israel circa 1947) are a handful of psalms

that were never included in any modern Bibles. This is further evidence that many "writings" were less than "official" as late as 200 C.E.

It does seem more likely, however, that the "Prophets" were thought to be canonical by most Jews during Jesus' time (including Joshua, Judges, 1 and 2 Samuel, 1 and 2 Kings, Isaiah, Jeremiah, Ezekiel, Hosea, Amos, Micah, Joel, Obadiah, Jonah, Nahum, Habakkuk, Zephaniah, Haggai, Zechariah, Malachi). Notice that the subheading "Prophets" would also have included many narratives as well. The books of Joshua, Judges, 1 and 2 Samuel, 1 and 2 Kings are often referred to as the "former prophets". The "latter prophets" would include Isaiah, Jeremiah, Ezekiel and also "the twelve" others.

Eventually the Jewish canon consisted of

Torah—Hebrew for "legal instruction"; also another way to refer to the five books of Moses (Pentateuch);
Nevi'im—Hebrew for "Prophets";
Ketuvim—Hebrews for "Writings".

The first letters of these three words (T, N, and K) form the acronym *TNK*. Today the Jewish biblical canon is called the "Tanakh" or "Tanak."

The Tanakh does not include any books of the New Testament. This leads many Christians to equate it with their Old Testament. While it is true that the Tanakh and the Old Testament share the same books, translations and uses will differ. Another important difference is how these two canons end. The Old Testament ends with Malachi 4:5-6: "Behold, I will send you Elijah the prophet before the great and terrible day of the LORD comes. And he will turn the hearts of fathers to their children and the hearts of children to their fathers, lest I come and smite the land with a curse." These final verses of the Old Testament suggest a need for repentance and a warning of a curse from the Lord. They also refer to the return of the prophet Elijah (who was believed to have escaped death and taken to heaven). This "ending" creates a problem to be solved by the New Testament. Indeed many early Christians believed that John the Baptist was "the Elijah who was to come" (Matthew 11:14). More importantly, both Jesus comes preaching repentance, as hoped for by Malachi. So from a Christian perspective, the Old Testament connects directly to the New Testament.

But the Tanakh ends with 2 Chronicles (not Malachi) and thus with an idealistic portrait of Israel's golden age. There is no great problem to be solved at the end of the Tanakh. It is complete. The Jewish books that come later are attempts to interpret, illuminate, and expand Scripture. These later Jewish texts are not a new "testament" as in Christian tradition. It is therefore not uncommon to hear the term "postbiblical period" used of the time of Jesus and the New Testament.

This simply illustrates the reality that the Bible is used differently, and is shaped differently, by different groups. Moreover it looks differently to different groups. As Dr. Sumney discusses in his textbook,

groups naturally create boundaries to maintain a sense of collective identity. *We are women. We support religious freedom. We root for the San Francisco Giants. We get together to watch Wes Anderson films. We stand up against human trafficking.* These are all statements that serve as boundary markers.

Many faith communities use the Bible (and patterns or styles of reading the Bible) as a boundary marker. *We take the Bible literally. We believe that the Bible arcs toward justice. We believe that Genesis teaches of six 24-hour days of creation. The Bible must be interpreted by the Church in order to be understood. We believe that the New Testament supersedes the Old Testament.* Such statements serve to mark off "insiders" from "outsiders." So not only does the Bible's official canon vary, the Bible is used differently from group to group. While we might say that the biblical canon is "closed" (in other words, very few groups are adding new books to their canon), the shape the Bible takes among worshipping communities is ever changing. And the reverse is true too: the Bible's shape helps to shape the group that reads it.

Questions for Group Discussion

1. Using the above description of canons alongside Sumney's discussion of the Apocrypha, which religious tradition do you think produced your copy of the Bible?
2. Which parts of the Bible do you think are most read by the groups you've encountered?
3. Read Proverbs 26:4 and then Proverbs 26:5; what does the fact that these two instructions are placed side by side say about the editor or collector of Proverbs?

Questions for Reflection

1. How might you think of the Gospel of Mark differently if you were certain the apostle Peter composed it?

2. How might you think of the Gospel of Mark differently if its author was completely anonymous?

3. Have you experience any incidences when the Bible was used to define "insiders" from "outsiders"? If so, how did you feel about this process?

2

From Then to Now:
The Transmission of the Bible

Summary and Learning Objectives

1. The Bible as it exists in our modern translations is the product of painstaking scholarship. Because we have no "original text" of the Bible, scholars evaluate the various copies and versions of the Bible from the ancient world. This is a process of reconstructing the books of the Bible based on various fragments, pages and versions of ancient manuscripts. After reading this chapter (alongside chapter 2 of Sumney's text), the reader should be able *to describe the various obstacles that scholars face as Textual Critics.*

2. Scholars who attempt to reconstruct the books of the Bible use ancient manuscripts like the Chester Beatty Papyri, Codex Sinaiticus, and Codex Vaticanus to create a baseline for translation. These third- and (mostly) fourth-century copies are especially important for the reconstruction of the Greek New Testament. After reading this chapter (alongside chapter 2 of Sumney's text), the reader should be able *to describe the development of the New Testament through oral tradition and scribal practice.*

3. The books of the Bible that survive today are copies of copies of copies. While most of the differences from copy to copy are seemingly insignificant, some of these differences are quite important. After reading this chapter (alongside chapter 2 of Sumney's text), the reader should be able *to identify the major changes to Mark's longer ending and the Greek version of Genesis 4:4-7.*

4. Beyond the reconstruction of the Greek New Testament, the process of translation to English is fraught with complexity. After reading this chapter (alongside chapter 2 of Sumney's text), the reader should be able *to identify at least three difficulties in translating Matthew 16:16-18.*

Key Terms

Autograph The original writing from the hand of the author. None of these exist for biblical books, only copies of copies are extant.

Aramaic A Semitic language, very similar to ancient Hebrew (not to be confused with Arabic). A Syrian dialect that was used as a common language in the Near East from the sixth century B.C.E. Some portions of the Books of Daniel and Ezra were written in Aramaic. It is probably the language that Jesus and his disciples spoke most often.

Hebrew Bible The books of the Bible that were written in Hebrew and Aramaic (not to be confused with Arabic). They are the authoritative writings for Judaism and contain the same thirty-nine books as the Protestant Old Testament. The books, however, are in different orders in the two canons.

Masoretic Text The standard text of the Hebrew Bible that comes from the scholars known as the Masoretes who meticulously copied the text to preserve its integrity. They also added vowels and accents to make the text easier to read and understand.

Septuagint The Greek translation of the Hebrew Scriptures that began coming together in the second to third century B.C.E. Commonly abbreviated as LXX.

Textual criticism The field of biblical studies that tries to establish the earliest possible wording of the biblical texts. This discipline also is able to trace the ways theological ideas developed by noting how theology influenced copyists to make alterations in the biblical texts.

Key Themes

▶ the complexity of translating from language to language
▶ the problem of different versions
▶ capturing the ideas behind the words
▶ the process of shaping the Gospel of Mark orally and textually

Primary Text

Translations of Translations

Jesus says something very interesting to Peter (the leader among his disciples) in Matthew 16. It starts with Peter's famous confession of faith. Peter says, "You are the Christ!" In this statement of faith, Peter states what we (the readers) already know. You see, we found out that Jesus is the Christ (or Messiah) from the narrator in Matthew's first chapter. But Peter—as he exists in the storyline—only confirms this in chapter 16. The passage goes like this:

> [16] Simon Peter answered, "You are the Christ, the Son of the living God." [17] And Jesus said to him, "Blessed are you, Simon Barjona, because flesh and blood did not reveal this to you, but my Father who is in Heaven. [18] I also say to you that you are Peter, and upon this rock I will build my church; and the gates of Hades will not overpower it." (Matthew 15:16-18)

Take a moment to notice that the narrator knows that Simon will get his named changed to Peter before Jesus officially renames him in the storyline. In fact, the narrator has been calling him Peter since chapter 4. So, if we follow the storyline closely, we (the readers) know Peter's name before he does. We must imagine that when Jesus and his disciples were walking around Galilee together, this man was just called Simon (or *Shimon*). But Matthew has no problem using the name Simon Peter or just Peter before this episode of his official renaming. It would be a bit like making a movie of the life of hip hop musician "P. Diddy" and having the main character called by his stage name even before he takes the stage for the first time. P. Diddy's given name is Sean John Combs. But everyone in the movie theater would just think of the main character by his stage name. As Matthew is telling his story about Jesus and Peter years later, his audience would have probably just thought of Peter by his more popular name.

Notice also that Peter calls Jesus by the title Christ. Of course, Peter would have never said this. Christ is an English word and Peter didn't speak English. Our earliest copies of Matthew are written in Greek. In these Greek texts the title is *Christos*. But Peter probably didn't use this term either. Peter probably spoke in Aramaic. (Barjona is an Aramaic name meaning "son of John.") So we're looking at this passage through several filters. We're reading it in English, translated from various copies of Matthew in Greek, while listening to a narrator tell a story. In fact, it is quite possible that Matthew wrote in Hebrew. If so, we're reading a translation, of a translation, of a translation, and so on. ,

Notice also that Jesus says to Peter, "upon this rock I will build my church." Of course Jesus would never have said it like this. The term *church* didn't exist in Aramaic. Again, Matthew is using a term that wasn't used until much later for the benefit of his readers. Also the word *Hades* is Greek, referring to the underworld. Perhaps Jesus was referring to *Hades*, the Greek god of the underworld. But Jesus doesn't refer to Greek mythology any place else. So this is a problem! If Matthew did write in Hebrew, would he have had the Hebrew word for grave

(*sheol*) in mind? This is probably the word that fits best, but it might change the meaning of the concept! I hope that you can see how very complicated translation can be. Some words and concepts don't translate well.

Finally, Jesus names him Peter in Matthew 16:18. In the Greek text it sounds like *petros*. But, again, Jesus wouldn't have said it like this. Our best guess is that Jesus called him *Kephas* (Aramaic for "rock"). Really, Jesus was giving Peter a nickname, sort of like when Italians call boys named Rocco, "Rocky." In fact "Rocky" might be a really great translation for "Peter" in this context! This would be a better "dynamic" translation of the name (see Sumney's discussion on "formal correspondence vs. dynamic equivalence"). But if our translations called him Rocky, we readers wouldn't know who the character was. We've always known him as Peter, after all. Most translators just stick with the names that we're already familiar with. The narrator of Matthew was probably working with the same logic: It's best to use words that most people will understand. So we get words like *Christ*, *church*, and *Peter*, throughout the gospel that make the best sense for Greek-speaking readers fifty years after Jesus and Peter were gone.

It might make you wonder about how scholars reconstruct passages of the Bible to give us our translations. As you might imagine, the scholarly process of translation is quite complicated. These few observations of Matthew 16 only illustrate some of the many problems of translation. As you can see, the process of translation isn't just a simple English version of the Greek. Before we can do this, we must ask the question, *which version of the Greek should we use?*

One of the first steps in this process is gathering the "textual witnesses" for a given passage. In chapter 2 of Sumney, we learn of some of the sources for the Greek New Testament. These texts—usually on parchment or vellum—provide us with copies that "witness" to us. It might seem odd to call these ancient scraps and pages "witnesses" because they weren't written by anyone who witnessed Jesus or Peter or Paul or in the flesh. These are just copies of copies of copies. Indeed it is often difficult to tell which copies are best. Scholars who work to collect and judge the merits of these ancient copies are called *textual critics*. Sumney discusses textual criticism, and I will touch again on this topic below in my section called *From Telling to Text*. Before doing so it will be helpful to consider an example from Genesis 4.

After Adam and Eve leave the stage, the next key characters are two brothers: Abel and Cain. As the story goes, Abel was a herdsman and Cain was a farmer. Abel and Cain both brought gifts to the altar of the Lord. The tradition was to offer your first "fruits" to God in a ritual fire. For Abel—a herdsman—this meant an animal sacrifice; for Cain—a farmer—this meant a burnt offering of grain. In this story, the Lord favors one offering but not the other. Below I have provided two versions of Genesis 4:4-7. Both are English translations, but one follows the Hebrew version—the Masoretic Text, or "MT"; the other follows a Greek version—the Septuagint, or "LXX". Both of these traditions are very ancient. Our oldest fragments of the Greek Pentateuch come from about 200 years before Jesus. Similarly, our oldest Hebrew texts of the Pentateuch come from the same period (Hebrew fragments of this story have been found in the Dead Sea Scrolls and are very similar the version you will find in most modern translations).

GENESIS 4:4-7 (NRSV) from the Hebrew

4 and Abel for his part brought of the firstlings of his flock, their fat portions. And the Lord had regard for Abel and his offering,
5 but for Cain and his offering he had no regard. So Cain was very angry, and his countenance fell.

6 The Lord said to Cain, "Why are you angry, and why has your countenance fallen?

7 If you do well, will you not be accepted? And if you do not do well, sin is lurking at the door; its desire is for you, but you must master it."

GENESIS 4:4-7 (Brenton translation) from the Greek

4 And Abel also brought of the first born of his sheep and of his fatlings, and God looked upon Abel and his gifts,
5 but Cain and his sacrifices he regarded not, and Cain was exceedingly sorrowful and his countenance fell.

6 And the Lord God said to Cain, Why art thou become very sorrowful and why is thy countenance fallen?

7 Hast thou not sinned if thou hast brought it rightly, but not rightly divided it? be still, to thee shall be his submission, and thou shalt rule over him.

This last line, verse 7, is the most glaring difference between these two versions. But first notice that the Hebrew tradition portrays Cain as "angry" while the Greek tradition portrays him as "sorrowful." This minor change in vocabulary changes the way we understand Cain's motives! Later in the story, we learn that Cain kills his brother. But does he commit this crime out of rage or did he become sullen and calculate a strategy? Second, notice that the Greek tradition suggests that the grain was not divided properly. Does this mean that the type of offering wasn't the problem, rather it was the amount? Third, notice that in the Hebrew tradition, "sin" becomes a character in the story—a character that lurks and desires. It is an enemy that must be mastered, so says the Lord. But in the Greek, the Lord says something altogether different. The divine voice commands Cain to "be still." The Lord then tells Cain that someone (Abel?) will be set under Cain's authority: "You shall rule over him." Without the introduction of a new character, named "sin" (as in the Hebrew), the reader of the Greek tradition might think that the Lord is speaking of Abel. After all, Abel is the younger brother and would have been under the authority of Cain. Is the Lord telling Cain that he will come out on top in the end? Or is the Lord warning Cain not to succumb to anger and sin? Given what happens next the story (Cain's murder of Abel), these are very important details to get right!

This is the sort of difference in translation that fascinates scholars. We do our best to study both traditions carefully and explain both versions side by side. Did ancient Greek-speaking translators attempt to change the story so that it made more sense to them? Did they inherit a different version of this story? Or does the Greek represent a more ancient version of the story? If so, when and why did the Hebrew version of the text change? Whatever

our answers, translators have privileged the Masoretic Text (the Hebrew tradition) when drafting English translations.

As we saw with the stories of Peter's confession and Cain's offering, modern translators are faced with a complex task. And these are only two examples! But the student reading this should not be discouraged. I would encourage you to choose to be fascinated by the challenge, rather than upset by the lack of certainty involved in the process.

From Telling to Text

One of the guiding questions of the text critic is *which reconstruction best represents the original autograph?* In other words, when Zechariah sat down—crosslegged with a pen and pad on his lap—to write out his prophecies, what were the actual words on his page? As the word *autograph* suggests, many scholars imagine that some of the books of the Bible were written down originally in the prophet's own hand. But more often than not, this is not the case. For example, we know that Jeremiah used a professional scribe named Baruch to write for him. So Jeremiah did the *telling,* while his scribe did the *texting.* (But, as Sumney discusses in chapter 2, the Dead Sea Scrolls confirm that other authors added major sections to the book, making it much longer than the version we read in our translations.) So it may be better to think of the earliest forms of biblical books as "archetypes" rather than "autographs."

In many cases, the process of telling was much less direct. It is important to keep in mind that the Bible was composed in a world that was largely illiterate. Only a small fraction of the populace could write like Baruch, the scribe. Our most educated guess is that most of the "books" of the Bible were remembered and passed *orally* for generations. So while we imagine something like an autograph from

Paul—who would have dictated his words directly to his scribe or written in his own hand—we shouldn't necessarily imagine that a book like Mark's Gospel was dictated directly to a single scribe. It might be better to imagine Mark as beginning with a dramatic story performed by a professional storyteller. It might have remained an oral gospel for years before it was penned.

In chapter 2, we read about the complicated process by which the New Testament became a unified whole—including the work of ancient scribes and copyists all the way to modern translators. It should be said that even with such a long and complicated process, we might expect that the New Testament texts to differ more than they do. Most of the time, it seems that the changes to Greek New Testament involve grammar, spelling, vocabulary, and word order. But as Sumney discusses in chapter 2, Mark's longer ending represents a major change with significant impact on the way we read the story. There are a few such cases in the New Testament. I would, again, encourage students to choose to be fascinated by this process, not upset by the lack of certainty scholars offer. I would also reiterate a point that Sumney makes: when we compare the Masoretic Text of the Hebrew Bible (copied in the ninth century C.E.) to the Hebrew Bible in the Dead Sea Scrolls (copied before and during the time of Jesus, 200 B.C.E.–150 C.E.), we find a remarkably stable tradition. In other words, in the course of a thousand years, the changes to these books were mostly minimal! This reminds us that oral cultures held texts in high regard and attempted to remain faithful the traditions that they preserved. In most cases, they seem to have been quite successful.

Questions for Group Discussion

1. Read Genesis chapter 4. In the story of Cain and Abel, what hints are we given of Cain's primary motives for killing his brother?
2. Given that only a small fraction of ancient peoples were scribally literate, what sort of power do your think that scribes enjoyed?
3. By comparing the Hebrew Bible in the Dead Sea Scrolls to the Masoretic Text that was copied 1000 years later, we find remarkable correspondence. While there are a some major changes, the Hebrew Bible seems to have developed with stability. How should this fact relate to the four-century process of Mark's composition outlined above?

Questions for Reflection

1. Have you ever said or heard something and found the intended meaning was "lost" in translation?

2. Do the problems in translating Peter's confession of faith (Matthew 16:16-18) trouble you or fascinate you? Or, if not either of these, what is your response?

3. When you hear a joke that you've heard before. Do you generally think of it as "*that* joke" or do you think of it as "multiple versions of a joke"? What does this say about the difference between an oral story and a written story?

3

Inspiration: The Claim That God Speaks in a Text

Summary and Learning Objectives

1. The Bible is more than an ancient library, it is considered to be sacred by most who read it. For centuries, readers of the Bible have felt an encounter with the divine within the pages of the Bible. After reading this chapter (alongside chapter 3 of Sumney's text), the reader should be able *to explain the roots of the belief that the Bible is inspired.*

2. One of the key passages used to support a high view of scripture is 2 Timothy 3:16. While this Pauline verse does indeed support the concept of inspiration, it has been misunderstood by many readers. After reading this chapter (alongside chapter 3 of Sumney's text), the reader should be able *to better understand the concept of inspiration as a translation of the Greek term for "God breathed."*

3. Quite commonly the Bible—for those who hold it sacred—is read as if it were the very words of God. Indeed, God does have several speaking roles. But the Bible also conveys a very human perspective. After reading this chapter the reader should be able *to discuss how a biblical poem written from a human perspective might be used in a sacred context.*

4. Overlapping with ideas of inspiration, the Bible often functions as an authority. After reading this chapter the reader should be able *to discuss how a narrative might provide an effective voice of authority.*

Key Terms

Inerrant   Term used of Scripture to claim that it is without any mistakes of any kind (history, science, geography, and so on). Others use the term to signify that Scripture is without error in religious teaching, though it may not have all historical and scientific facts correct.

Inspiration   The belief that God was involved with the writing and reading of the Bible.

21

Lament psalms   Psalms that mourn a personal or national loss or defeat.

Key Themes

▶ The human voices within sacred texts

▶ The Bible in story form

▶ The vitality and holiness of the breath of God

Primary Text

God's Word in Human Words

In the simplest terms, God is the main character of the Bible. With Esther as the only exception, God is mentioned in every book of the Bible. In many books God has speaking roles; the "divine voice" speaks forth from burning bushes, tornadoes, from the heavens, and so on. Primarily, the Bible is a book about God. But no story that is worth telling is without problems. Unless the main character experiences some drama, the story is uninteresting. Of equal importance is the setting and relationships that surround the main character. We might think of Israel as God's great love and the cosmos as the stage. Some have even said that the Bible is like a series of passionate letters sent between two lovers. Sometimes we overhear great affection; sometimes we overhear heated spats.

Although this view of the Bible has limits, it is helpful in that it reminds us that we're hearing multiple voices in conversation. In addition to hearing the divine voice, the Bible also provides a distinctly *human* perspective. Consider this passage from Psalm 44. The poet is talking about Israel's collective gratitude to God: "In God we have boasted continually, and we will give thanks to your name forever." This sounds very much like a love letter. But the tone turns sour as the psalm continues. I have emphasized a few important phrases in bold:

> [11] You have made us like sheep for slaughter
>   and have scattered us among the nations.
> [12] You have **sold your people for a trifle,**
>   demanding no high price for them.
> [13] You have made us the taunt of our neighbors,
>   the derision and scorn of those around us.
> [14] You have made us a byword among the nations,
>   a laughingstock among the peoples.
> [15] All day long my disgrace is before me,
>   and shame has covered my face
> [16] at the words of the taunters and revilers,
>   at the sight of the enemy and the avenger.
> [17] All this has come upon us,
>   **yet we have not forgotten you,**
>   or been false to your covenant.
> [18] Our heart has not turned back,
>   nor have our steps departed from your way,
> [19] yet you have broken us in the haunt of jackals,
>   and covered us with deep darkness.
> [20] If we had forgotten the name of our God,
>   or spread out our hands to a strange god,
> [21] would not God discover this?
>   For he knows the secrets of the heart.
> [22] Because of you we are being killed all day long,
>   and accounted as sheep for the slaughter.
> [23] **Rouse yourself! Why do you sleep, O Lord?**
>   Awake, do not cast us off forever!
> [24] Why do you hide your face?
>   **Why do you forget** our affliction and oppression?
> [25] For we sink down to the dust;
>   our bodies cling to the ground.

²⁶ Rise up, come to our help.

Redeem us for the sake of your steadfast
love.

(Psalm 44:11-26)

This final line reveals the belief that God does in fact love Israel. But it is a desperate plea for God to remember! The poet, speaking for Israel, accuses God of selling them into slavery. As if this wasn't bad enough, God seems to have sold them cheaply! This kind of accusation is not unheard of in Israel's tradition. This poem is called a lament psalm and such psalms often express disappointment, grief, or anger. What is remarkable in this psalm—actually quite surprising—is that the poet claims that Israel has *not* forgotten God or been unfaithful in any way. Rather, Israel is innocent and God is at fault! According to this psalm, God is negligent, forgetful, and perhaps even sleeping while Israel is close to death.

I often read this psalm to my students and ask a rhetorical question: *does this poem offer a divine perspective or a human perspective?* This question is rhetorical because the answer is obvious. This poem reads like a letter from a forgotten orphan to a deadbeat dad. Yet for millennia, lament psalms (including this one) have been considered sacred. Many people (billions, in fact) would consider this psalm to be divinely inspired. It is not my intention to contradict this belief. What I would suggest is that any understanding of inspiration must be able to explain passages like we find in Psalm 44. For those who believe that this poem is the "Word of God" must also acknowledge that the Word of God includes the words of humans. This perspective may make some people uncomfortable and this is understandable. I simply encourage my students to give some thought to what the Bible *is* by reading what the Bible *says*.

According to a Pauline perspective, "All scripture is inspired by God and is useful for teaching, for reproof, for correction, and for training in righteousness." Sumney discusses this verse—2 Timothy 3:16—at length in his third chapter. He is quite right when he reminds us that in the first century C.E. (when 2 Timothy was written) there wasn't yet a New Testament, as it was still under construction. In this case, "scripture" refers most directly to the Hebrew Bible, or a Greek translation of it. This, of course, would include lament psalms. In support of this Pauline view of inspiration, I would affirm that Psalm 44 can indeed be "useful for teaching, for reproof, for correction, and for training." Allow me to provide an example. There is a monument to the Holocaust in Göttingen, Germany. It commemorates the six million Jews who were dehumanized and then murdered during World War II. There are many such monuments throughout the world, but this particular monument quotes Psalm 44. Perhaps in the face of hopelessness, Psalm 44 is indeed useful. One of the virtues of lament psalms is that they provide appropriate space to reprove God. If so, something sacred would be lost if we failed to hear the distinctly human perspectives in the Bible.

God Breathed

In chapter three of Sumney's text, and also here, 2 Timothy 3:16 has been discussed. It is an important verse because the doctrine of inspiration is important to most readers of the Bible. It is also an interesting verse in that it contains a very strange Greek word: *theopneustos*. A literal translation of this word would be "God-breathed." So this verse claims that Scripture is breathed by God. This word reminds us that the breath of God is very important in Jewish tradition. God's breath (or wind, or spirit) is an extension of God as creator, who gives life. With this in mind consider this passage from Genesis 2:7-8:

> ... then the LORD God formed the human from the dust of the ground, and breathed into his nostrils the breath of life; and the human became a living being. [8] And the LORD God planted a garden in Eden, in the east; and there he put the man whom he had formed.

The idea here is that God, as creator, breathed his very spirit into humankind to give it life. Consider also this passage from the end of John's Gospel. In this story, Jesus has risen from the dead and is about to give his disciples divine authority. John 20:21-22:

> "Peace be with you. As the Father has sent me, so I send you." [22] When he had said this, he breathed on them and said to them, "Receive the Holy Spirit..."

Reminiscent of God's breath in Genesis 2, this passage describes Jesus breathing forth the Holy Spirit onto his disciples. The key concept here is that Jesus is giving them new life. In both Genesis and John, the divine breath is given to humans. We might also observe that in both cases these humans are also given authority and instructions.

While it is a bit strange for 2 Timothy to claim that scriptures (not living beings) are God-breathed, Genesis 2 and John 20 might give us a good framework to understand biblical "inspiration." In relationship to a creative God, a part of creation can be made vital and holy. In Genesis 2, humanity is made vital (infused with life) and holy (given a sacred purpose). In John 20, the apostles are made vital (infused with life) and holy (given a sacred purpose). Perhaps 2 Timothy 3:16 is claiming something similar of Jewish scripture.

But consider this: whatever "God-breathed" means, it doesn't seem to mean "without error." (After all, the Bible describes God's breath "inspiring" human beings without making them infallible. The vital breath of God did not ensure that Adam would not err. Adam makes an archetypal error in Genesis 3! And the vital breath of Jesus does not ensure that the apostles will not err. Peter is famous for his mistakes—especially in his life *after* receiving the Holy Spirit: see Galatians 2:11.) To say that scripture is God-breathed, or inspired, does not equate to being "without error" as many modern Christians have argued. This is a doctrine that emerged quite late in the history of Christianity (see A. A. Hodge, *Outlines of Theology* [New York, Scribner, 1879] for one of the first formulations of this doctrine). Finally, to my mind, to say that the Bible is *vital* and *holy* is a much stronger statement than saying it is simply *without error.*

Authority

While the argument for biblical inerrancy is relatively recent, the claim that the Jewish and Christians scriptures are authoritative is ancient. As we saw in chapter 1, the legal instructions and stories most associated with Moses became vital and holy for Israel. Similarly, the writings most associated with the apostles became the most vital and holy for Christianity. In both cases, relating a text to a great leader brought a definite authority to the text. It is not unlike modern political appeals to the ideals of "founding fathers."

We see a similar move with the legacy of Solomon. King Solomon is remembered as a conduit of divine wisdom. Because of this reputation, all sorts of poems and songs were attributed to him. 1 Kings 4:32 claims that Solomon wrote "1005 songs." But the Greek translation of this passage claims that "his songs were 5000" (4:32, LXX). No doubt, the Greek translation has exaggerated the number. It is also true that the number of songs, poems, and books that were attributed to Solomon increased over time. Many modern readers still assume that Ecclesiastes was written by Solomon. Very few scholars support this view and (importantly) the book of Ecclesiastes does not claim to be written by Solomon. It is simply our tendency to associate biblical wisdom literature with a great, wise king. The key virtue of this is that Solomon is reputed to have a direct access to godly wisdom and therefore his writings carry authority (see 1 Kings 3).

So it is traditional to view scriptures as possessing authority. There are, of course, varying Jewish and Christian ideas of authority. Many treat the Bible as a selection of prescriptions and prohibitions dictated from on high. No doubt, the Bible does contain legal instructions and rules that govern life in society. But the Bible gives us various clues about how we should read these rules. Allow me to highlight just one of these clues: the Ten Commandments (the famous ten rules, primary to Israelite life and worship) are part of a longer narrative. These exist within a story of liberation and embrace. In Exodus, God has liberated Israel from slavery and embraced her. The Ten Commandments given to Moses must be read as a part of this redemptive story. Importantly, it is the *story*—the whole story—that carries the authority. So I would ask: *in what way can a story be authoritative?*

Christian scholar N. T. Wright has an interesting answer to this question. He suggests a hypothetical scenario involving an army captain and his troops. Imagine that a regiment of troops are lined up attentively and waiting for their orders. But when their captain arrives he invites them to sit down and tells them a story. At the end of the story the captain says, "go, then, and live like this." My guess is that this sort of army wouldn't win many battles. But the Bible functions much like this for people who read it as a sacred text. In many ways, stories (like that

of Exodus) can be better instructional guides than direct commands. For example, suggests Wright,

> A familiar story told with a new twist in the tail jolts people into thinking differently about themselves and the world. A story told with pathos, humor, or drama opens the imagination and invites readers and hearers to imagine themselves in similar situations, offering new insights about God and human beings which enable them then to order their own lives more wisely.
>
> Source: N. T. Wright, *Scripture and the Authority of God: How to Read the Bible Today* (New York: HarperOne, 2005), 25.

It is important to realize that Wright's position is not a liberal or even contemporary move. This is a very old understanding of biblical instruction. Christians who attempt to reduce the Bible to a book of rules are the latecomers to this conversation. And, for what it's worth, Wright's voice is that of a faithful Christian. To fill out this discussion, consider the view of Marc Zvi Brettler, who is an observant Jewish scholar. For Brettler, the Bible is "a sourcebook that I—within my community—make into a textbook. I do so by selecting, revaluing, and interpreting the texts that I call sacred." (*How to Read the Bible* [Philadelphia: Jewish Publication Society, 2005], 280.) Brettler is careful to point out that his view does not represent Judaism generally. Brettler does, however, represent many biblical scholars who also worship within communities that hold the Bible as sacred. Also notice that in Brettler's view, the Bible has a particular function within his community. It does not stand above and dictate from on high. Rather the Bible is something to be read and discussed in a collective way.

Finally, students of the Bible should be aware that many of their conversation partners do not hold the Bible as sacred, inspired, or authoritative. The scholarly worktable should be a hospitable place where all voices are welcomed. In order to have the most robust and fruitful conversation possible, we ought to be able to discuss the Bible in such a way that does not alienate our neighbors.

Questions for Group Discussion

1. How is God portrayed in Psalm 44? Does this portrait trouble you?
2. In both Genesis 2 and John 20, people receive a breath of divine inspiration. How does this help us understand the status of being "God breathed"?
3. How do the views of N. T. Wright and Marc Zvi Brettler on the authority of the Bible differ?

Questions for Reflection

1. What have been your impressions of the Bible? Have you thought of it as holy, inerrant, inspired, or authoritative? Has your understanding changed over the years?

2. What is the difference between saying that the Bible is "without error" and saying that it is "inspired"?

4

The Pentateuch, Part 1: Genesis

Summary and Learning Objectives

1. The Bible is not a science textbook, nor a factual report. A close reading of Genesis 1 reveals that something deeper, more profound and artistic is being conveyed. After reading this chapter (alongside chapter 4 of Sumney's text), the reader should be able *to identify at least three poetic features of Genesis 1.*

2. A valuable tool used by biblical scholars is cultural analysis by way of comparison. It is often helpful to compare the stories and poetry of the Bible with that of neighboring cultures. After reading this chapter (alongside chapter 4 of Sumney's text), the reader should be able *to recognize multiple parallels between Israel's worship and ritual practice and that of their Mesopotamian neighbors.*

3. In Genesis, God seems to favor certain people and choose them over others. These stories lay the groundwork for Israel's relational contract (or covenant) with the Lord. After reading this chapter, the reader should be able *to identify a few key features to contractual rituals in the ancient Mesopotamian world.*

Key Terms

Abraham The originating ancestor of Jews and Arabs in Genesis. God called him from his home region of Ur to travel to Canaan, which would become the homeland of his descendants. His original name was Abram.

Election Being chosen. In the Hebrew Bible, the Israelites are God's chosen people. New Testament writers also attach this designation to those who come to belief in Christ, in addition to those in the Mosaic covenant.

Enuma Elish   A twelfth-century (or earlier) B.C.E. Babylonian text that gives an account of the creation of the earth by many gods.

Gilgamesh, Epic of   A document composed around 2000 B.C.E. in Sumerian that includes a story of Gilgamesh building an ark in which he and the animals survive a worldwide flood.

Parallelism   A literary technique used in Hebrew poetry that thematically and structurally links two or more lines.

Key Themes

- ▶ God's pursuit of and plan for Israel
- ▶ God's promises to bless and favor Abraham
- ▶ Israel's identity as a people liberated from slavery

Primary Text

Genesis 1:1—2:3

The first chapter of the Bible is a poem. It may not look it in English, but Genesis 1:2—2:3 is poetic verse. Hebrew poetry is structured in parallel verses. Sometimes this "parallelism" is a simple two verses, one right after the other. The first poem in Genesis is much more elaborate and elegant. As you read the following verses, try to notice repeated words and phrases.

> [1] In the beginning when God created the heavens and the earth, [2] the earth was a formless void and darkness covered the face of the deep, while a wind from God swept over the face of the waters. [3] Then God said, "Let there be light"; and there was light. [4] And God saw that the light was good; and

God separated the light from the darkness. [5] God called the light Day, and the darkness he called Night. And there was evening and there was morning, the first day.

[6] And God said, "Let there be a dome in the midst of the waters, and let it separate the waters from the waters." [7] So God made the dome and separated the waters that were under the dome from the waters that were above the dome. And it was so. [8] God called the dome Sky. And there was evening and there was morning, the second day.

[9] And God said, "Let the waters under the sky be gathered together into one place, and let the dry land appear." And it was so. [10] God called the dry land Earth, and the waters that were gathered together he called Seas. And God saw that it was good. [11] Then God said, "Let the earth put forth vegetation: plants yielding seed, and fruit trees of every kind on earth that bear fruit with the seed in it." And it was so. [12] The earth brought forth vegetation: plants yielding seed of every kind, and trees of every kind bearing fruit with the seed in it. And God saw that it was good. [13] And there was evening and there was morning, the third day.

[14] And God said, "Let there be lights in the dome of the sky to separate the day from the night; and let them be for signs and for seasons and for days and years, [15] and let them be lights in the dome of the sky to give light upon the earth." And it was so. [16] God made the two great lights—the greater light to rule the day and the lesser light to rule the night—and the stars. [17] God set them in the dome of the sky to give

light upon the earth, [18] to rule over the day and over the night, and to separate the light from the darkness. And God saw that it was good. [19] And there was evening and there was morning, the fourth day.

[20] And God said, "Let the waters bring forth swarms of living creatures, and let birds fly above the earth across the dome of the sky." [21] So God created the great sea monsters and every living creature that moves, of every kind, with which the waters swarm, and every winged bird of every kind. And God saw that it was good. [22] God blessed them, saying, "Be fruitful and multiply and fill the waters in the seas, and let birds multiply on the earth." [23] And there was evening and there was morning, the fifth day.

[24] And God said, "Let the earth bring forth living creatures of every kind: cattle and creeping things and wild animals of the earth of every kind." And it was so. [25] God made the wild animals of the earth of every kind, and the cattle of every kind, and everything that creeps upon the ground of every kind. And God saw that it was good.

[26] Then God said, "Let us make humankind in our image, according to our likeness; and let them have dominion over the fish of the sea, and over the birds of the air, and over the cattle, and over all the wild animals of the earth, and over every creeping thing that creeps upon the earth."

[27] So God created humankind in his image,

in the image of God he created them;
male and female he created them.

[28] God blessed them, and God said to them, "Be fruitful and multiply, and fill the earth and subdue it; and have dominion over the fish of the sea and over the birds of the air and over every living thing that moves upon the earth." [29] God said, "See, I have given you every plant yielding seed that is upon the face of all the earth, and every tree with seed in its fruit; you shall have them for food. [30] And to every beast of the earth, and to every bird of the air, and to everything that creeps on the earth, everything that has the breath of life, I have given every green plant for food." And it was so. [31] God saw everything that he had made, and indeed, it was very good. And there was evening and there was morning, the sixth day.

2 [1] Thus the heavens and the earth were finished, and all their multitude. [2] And on the seventh day God finished the work that he had done, and he rested on the seventh day from all the work that he had done. [3] So God blessed the seventh day and hallowed it, because on it God rested from all the work that he had done in creation. (Genesis 1:1–2:3)

Now consider this outline of the poem. Notice the patterns of "filling" and "separating." Notice also that days one and four link together topically. Similar parallels can be found in days two and five, and then days three and six:

A1. Day 1—God separates (1:3-5)
   a. light
   b. dark
   A2. Day 2—God separates (1:6-8)
      a. water
      b. sky
      A3. Day 3—God separates (1:9-13)
         a. land
         b. plants spring up from the land
B1. Day 4—God fills (1:14-19)
   a. the light with the sun
   b. the dark with the moon
   B2. Day 5—God fills (1:20-23)
      a. the water with fish
      b. the sky with birds
      B3. Day 6—God fills (1:24-31)
         a. the land with animals and humans
         b. the plants are given as food
C. Day 7—God finishes his separating and filling and sits down on the seventh day (2:1-3)

A Sumerian Creation Story

This reading is a section that tells of the creation of humans. Notice what the purpose of humans is said to be.

> In those days, in the days when heaven and earth were created; in those nights, in the nights when heaven and earth were created; in those years, in the years when the fates were determined; when the Anuna gods were born; when the goddesses were taken in marriage; when the goddesses were distributed in heaven and earth; when the goddesses . . . . . . became pregnant and gave birth; when the gods were obliged (?) . . . . . . their food . . . . . . dining halls; the senior gods oversaw the work, while the minor gods were bearing the toil. The gods were digging the canals and piling up the silt in Ḫarali. The gods, crushing the clay, began complaining about this life.
>
> At that time, the one of great wisdom, the creator of all the senior gods, Enki lay on his bed, not waking up from his sleep, in the deep engur, in the subterranean water, the place the inside of which no other god knows. The gods said, weeping: "He is the cause of the lamenting!" Namma, the primeval mother who gave birth to the senior gods, took the tears of the gods to the one who lay sleeping, to the one who did not wake up from his bed, to her son: "Are you really lying there asleep, and . . . . not awake? The gods, your creatures, are smashing their . . . . . . My son, wake up from your bed! Please apply the skill deriving from your wisdom and create a substitute (?) for the gods so that they can be freed from their toil!" . . . And after Enki, the fashioner of designs by himself, had pondered the matter, he said to his mother Namma: "My mother, the creature you planned will really come into existence. Impose on him the work of carrying baskets [to feed the gods]. (*Enki and Ninmaḫ*: c.1.1.2)

What other parallels do you see between this text and Genesis chapters 1 and 2?

The Creation of the World from Ancient Babylon

Here is another creation myth older than Genesis.

1.   When Marduk heard the word of the gods
2.   His heart prompted him and he devised [a cunning plan].

3. He opened his mouth and unto Ea [he spake],

4. [That which] he had conceived in his heart he imparted [unto him]:

5. "My blood will I take and bone will I [fashion],

6. "I will make man, that man may . . . [. . .].

7. "I will create man who shall inhabit [the earth],"

8. "That the service of the gods may be established, and that [their] shrines [may be built]. (*Enuma Elish* Tablet 6.1-8)

How does the purpose of humans here compare with what is said of them in Genesis?

Genesis 3

Genesis 3 is often called "the Fall" by theologians. This story has captured the fascination of western culture because it attempts to explain the problems of humanity and to set a divine drama in motion. Notice the many difference between the "serpent" in this passage and the serpents you encounter in other literature (and experience).

[1] Now the serpent was more crafty than any other wild animal that the Lord God had made. He said to the woman, "Did God say, 'You shall not eat from any tree in the garden'?" [2] The woman said to the serpent, "We may eat of the fruit of the trees in the garden; [3] but God said, 'You shall not eat of the fruit of the tree that is in the middle of the garden, nor shall you touch it, or you shall die.' " [4] But the serpent said to the woman, "You will not die; [5] for God knows that when you eat of it your eyes will be opened, and you will be like God, knowing good and evil." [6] So when the woman saw that the tree was good for food, and that it was a delight to the eyes, and that

the tree was to be desired to make one wise, she took of its fruit and ate; and she also gave some to her husband, who was with her, and he ate. [7] Then the eyes of both were opened, and they knew that they were naked; and they sewed fig leaves together and made loincloths for themselves.

[8] They heard the sound of the Lord God walking in the garden at the time of the evening breeze, and the man and his wife hid themselves from the presence of the Lord God among the trees of the garden. [9] But the Lord God called to the man, and said to him, "Where are you?" [10] He said, "I heard the sound of you in the garden, and I was afraid, because I was naked; and I hid myself." [11] He said, "Who told you that you were naked? Have you eaten from the tree of which I commanded you not to eat?" [12] The man said, "The woman whom you gave to be with me, she gave me fruit from the tree, and I ate." [13] Then the Lord God said to the woman, "What is this that you have done?" The woman said, "The serpent tricked me, and I ate." [14] The Lord God said to the serpent,

"Because you have done this,
    cursed are you among all animals
    and among all wild creatures;
upon your belly you shall go,
    and dust you shall eat
    all the days of your life.
[15] I will put enmity between you and the woman,
    and between your offspring and hers;
he will strike your head,
    and you will strike his heel."

[16] To the woman he said,

"I will greatly increase your pangs in
        childbearing;
    in pain you shall bring forth children,
yet your desire shall be for your husband,
    and he shall rule over you."

[17] And to the man he said,

"Because you have listened to the voice of your
        wife,
    and have eaten of the tree
about which I commanded you,
    'You shall not eat of it,'
cursed is the ground because of you;
    in toil you shall eat of it all the days of
        your life;
[18] thorns and thistles it shall bring forth for
    you;
    and you shall eat the plants of the field.
[19] By the sweat of your face
    you shall eat bread
until you return to the ground,
    for out of it you were taken;
you are dust,
    and to dust you shall return."

[20] The man named his wife Eve, because she was the mother of all who live. [21] And the Lord God made garments of skins for the man and for his wife, and clothed them.

[22] Then the Lord God said, "See, the man has become like one of us, knowing good and evil; and now, he might reach out his hand and take also from the tree of life, and eat, and live for ever"—[23] therefore the Lord God sent him forth from the garden of Eden, to till the ground from which he was taken. [24] He drove out the man; and at the east of the garden of Eden he placed the cherubim, and a sword flaming and turning to guard the way to the tree of life. (Genesis 3:1-24)

A Fall story in the Epic of Gilgamesh

In this passage, Gilgamesh fears the power of Enkidu, a hero who lives with the animals. So he decides to weaken Enkidu by making him someone whom the animals will fear. He does this by sending a prostitute to seduce him. Note what the result is in relation to the animals and what the woman says he has become. Compare this with the Genesis story. Think of both what Adam and Eve are offered and what the act is that brings their fall (Gen. 3:3-6). Think also about what their act does to their relationship with nature (Gen. 3:14-19).

Then [came] Enkidu, whose home was the
        mountains,
who with gazelles ate herbs,
and with the cattle slaked his thirst,
and with the creatures of the waters rejoiced
        his heart.
And Shamhat, the enticer of men, saw him * * *
"Behold, there he is" (the hunter exclaimed);
    "now disclose your womb,
uncover your nakedness, and let him enjoy
        your favors.
Be not ashamed, but yield to his sensuous lust.
He shall see you and shall approach you;
Remove your garment, and he shall lie in your
        arms;
satisfy his desire after the manner of women;
then his cattle, raised with him on the field,
        will forsake him
while he firmly presses his breast upon yours."

And Shamhat disclosed her womb, uncovered
   her nakedness, and let him enjoy her
   favors.
She was not ashamed, but yielded to his sensuous lust.
She removed her garment, he lay in her arms,
and she satisfied his desire after the manner of
   women.
He pressed his breast firmly upon hers.
For six days and seven nights Enkidu enjoyed
   the love of Shamhat.
And when he had sated himself with her
   charms,
he turned his countenance toward his cattle.
The gazelles, resting, beheld Enkidu; they and
the cattle of the field turned away from him.
This startled Enkidu and his body grew faint;
his knees became stiff, as his cattle departed,
and he became less agile than ever before.
And as he listened, he made a resolve.
He turned again, in love enthralled, to the feet
   of the harlot,
and gazed up into the face of the ensnarer.
And while the ensnarer spoke, his ears listened
   attentively;
and the siren spoke to Enkidu and said:
"Lofty are you, Enkidu, you shall be like a
   god; Why, then, do you lie down with the
   beasts of the field?"

Source: William Muss-Arnolt, "The Gilgamesh
Narrative, Usually Called the Babylonian Nim-
rod Epic," in *Assyrian and Babylonian Litera-*
ture: Selected Translations, ed. Robert Francis
Harper (New York: D. Appleton and Co., 1901),
with slight revisions.

Genesis 15

In this ancient world, many people believed the
accumulation of power and wealth (and many

children) were proof that the gods favored you and
your clan. Many of Israel's most important stories
subvert power expectations. The God of Israel is the
sort of god who will sometimes favor a wandering
people, a lesser clan, a younger brother, and so on.
With this in mind, consider this important passage
from Genesis 15:

[1] . . . Lord came to Abram in a vision, "Do
not be afraid, Abram, I am your shield;
your reward shall be very great." [2] But
Abram said, "O Lord God, what will you
give me, for I continue childless, and the
heir of my house is Eliezer of Damascus?"
[3] And Abram said, "You have given me no
offspring, and so a slave born in my house
is to be my heir." [4] But the word of the Lord
came to him, "This man shall not be your
heir; no one but your very own issue shall
be your heir." [5] He brought him outside and
said, "Look toward heaven and count the
stars, if you are able to count them." Then
he said to him, "So shall your descendants
be." [6] And he believed the Lord; and the
Lord reckoned it to him as righteousness.
[7] Then he said to him, "I am the Lord who
brought you from Ur of the Chaldeans, to
give you this land to possess." [8] But he said,
"O Lord God, how am I to know that I shall
possess it?" [9] He said to him, "Bring me a
heifer three years old, a female goat three
years old, a ram three years old, a turtle-
dove, and a young pigeon." [10] He brought
him all these and cut them in two, laying
each half over against the other . . . [13] Then
the Lord said to Abram, "Know this for certain, that your offspring shall be aliens in a
land that is not theirs, and shall be slaves
there, and they shall be oppressed for four

hundred years; [14] but I will bring judgment on the nation that they serve, and afterward they shall come out with great possessions." (Genesis 15:1-14)

This passage is called the "Abrahamic Covenant." Notice that Abraham's fortunes are changed in several ways. Abraham (called Abram here) is not without wealth, but he lacks land and children. What else does God promise Abraham? Notice also the use of animals in the ritual of the treaty.

In ancient Mesopotamia, a common way of making a covenant or treaty was for the parties to walk between the parts of the bodies of animals that had been severed in two. The ritual basically invited the gods to do to you what had been done to the animals if you fail to live up to your part of the covenant. In the literature of ancient Mari, they often used a young donkey. The practice was common enough that "killing a donkey" was a way of referring to ratifying a covenant.

Questions for Group Discussion

1. How do the many parallels between Genesis and other ancient texts help us understand the genre of the Bible?
2. In the first two chapters in Genesis, humankind is given a place of honor above the rest of animal life. What does this suggest about the status of the serpent in Genesis 3?
3. The Lord's words to Abram in Genesis 15 look forward to 400 years of slavery. Why do you think that this topic comes up in the context of covenant?

Questions for Reflection

1. Does knowing that Genesis chapter 1 is a poem enhance your reading experience? Does it change the way you think about it?

2. What are the fundamental differences between the God and people of Genesis and those of the other ancient texts mentioned above?

5

The Pentateuch, Part 2:
Exodus through Deuteronomy

Summary and Learning Objectives

1. The story of the Exodus includes the life of Moses, Israel's liberation from slavery, their long sojourn in the wilderness, their accumulation of their legal instructions and life ethics. The memory of the Exodus is foundational in their emergence as a nation. After reading this chapter (alongside chapter 5 of Sumney's text), the reader should be able *to identify several key episodes that make up the Exodus narrative.*

2. Moses is among the most complex characters in the Bible. He has a multifaceted legacy and his personality development is among the most interesting in western literature. After reading this chapter (alongside chapter 5 of Sumney's text), the reader should be able *to recount at least three stories from Moses' life.*

3. Exodus, Leviticus, Numbers, and Deuteronomy are among the most important books of the Bible. After reading this chapter (alongside chapter 5 of Sumney's text), the reader should be able *to speak to at least five key cultural elements at work behind these legal texts.*

Key Terms

Exodus The story of the Israelites escaping slavery in Egypt. This story becomes the foundational story for their understanding of themselves and God.

Holiness Code Leviticus 17–26, the section that defines the ways the people of Israel are to live so that they are holy, pleasing God and different from the peoples around them.

Levirate marriage A system designed to keep property within a clan. In this system, when a man dies without children, his brother is to marry the dead man's wife and have children in the name of the dead man so that there are heirs to inherit the family property.

Tabernacle Portable worship structure described in Exodus that served as the temple for God while the Israelites were in the wilderness.

Key Themes

▶ God's power, but also God's flexibility

▶ God's willingness to listen to suffering and complaint

▶ Leadership dynamics

▶ What does a just society look like?

Primary Text

Birth stories of leaders

Exodus 2:1-7 tells the story of the birth of Moses. It might be helpful to remember that the Hebrew word for "basket" is the same used of the ark in Genesis six. This reminds us of Moses' mortal danger as he floated down the river.

[1] Now a man from the house of Levi went and married a Levite woman. [2] The woman conceived and bore a son; and when she saw that he was a fine baby, she hid him three months. [3] When she could hide him no longer she got a papyrus basket for him, and plastered it with bitumen and pitch; she put the child in it and placed it among the reeds on the bank of the river. [4] His sister stood at a distance, to see what would happen to him.

[5] The daughter of Pharaoh came down to bathe at the river, while her attendants walked beside the river. She saw the basket among the reeds and sent her maid to bring it. [6] When she opened it, she saw the child. He was crying, and she took pity on him, "This must be one of the Hebrews' children," she said. [7] Then his sister said to Pharaoh's daughter, "Shall I go and get you a nurse from the Hebrew women to nurse the child for you?" (Exodus 2:1-7)

Compare the story of the birth of Moses to the following account of the birth of Sargon of Agade (c. 2234–2279 B.C.E.). Keep in mind that this legend predates the story of Moses:

> My lowly mother conceived me, in secret she brought me forth.
> She set me in a basket of rushes, with bitumen she closed my door;
> she cast me into the river, which (rose) not over me.
> The river bore me up, unto Akki, the irrigator it carried me.
> Akki, the irrigator, with . . . [. . .] lifted me out,
> Akki, the irrigator, as his own son reared me.

Source: L. W. King, trans., "The Legend of Sargon, 1.5-10," in *Chronicles Concerning Early Babylonian Kings*, vol. 2. (London: Luzac and Co., 1907.)

What do such stories say about the person who is born? Do either of these stories suggest some sort of divine involvement or favor?

Shoes and the presence of God

A "theophany" is a religious experience wherein a person witnesses God. Moses' encounter with the burning bush is among the most famous theophanies. Exodus 3:1-6 describes Moses coming into God's presence:

[1] Moses was keeping the flock of his father-in-law Jethro, the priest of Midian; he led

his flock beyond the wilderness, and came to Horeb, the mountain of God. ² There the angel of the Lord appeared to him in a flame of fire out of a bush; he looked, and the bush was blazing, yet it was not consumed. ³ Then Moses said "I must turn aside and look at this great sight, and see why the bush is not burned up." ⁴ When the Lord saw that he had turned aside to see, God called to him out of the bush, "Moses, Moses!" And he said, "Here I am." ⁵ Then he said, "Come no closer! Remove the sandals from your feet, for the place on which you are standing is holy ground." ⁶ He said further, "I am the God of your father, the God of Abraham, the God of Isaac, and the God of Jacob." And Moses hid his face, for he was afraid to look at God.

In the following passage, Justin Martyr (written centuries after Exodus), describes pagan worship.

[H]aving heard this washing published by the prophet [Moses], [they] instigated those who enter their temples, and are about to approach them with libations and burnt-offerings, also to sprinkle themselves; and they cause them also to wash themselves entirely, as they depart [from the sacrifice], before they enter into the shrines in which their images are set. And the command, too, given by the priests to those who enter and worship in the temples, that they take off their shoes. (*Apology* 1.62)

Notice the common element in these descriptions. What does that suggest about rituals followed when approaching a god in the ancient world?

Code of Hammurabi and the Mosaic Law

Ancient cultures had different notions than ours about what it meant to treat people humanely. In many cases, "might made right," making stolen property, violence, and slavery common. It is then not surprising to see legal instructions emerge to create a more tolerable society. Exodus provides a window into ancient ethics. You'll see that slavery and violence are widespread realities that the writers of Exodus are attempting to regulate:

²² When people who are fighting injure a pregnant woman so that there is a miscarriage, and yet no further harm follows, the one responsible shall be fined what the woman's husband demands, paying as much as the judges determine. ²³ If any harm follows, then you shall give life for life, ²⁴ eye for eye, tooth for tooth, hand for hand, foot for foot, ²⁵ burn for burn, wound for wound, stripe for stripe.

²⁶ When a slave-owner strikes the eye of a male or female slave, destroying it, the owner shall let the slave go, a free person, to compensate for the eye. ²⁷ If the owner knocks out a tooth of a male or female slave, the slave shall be let go, a free person, to compensate for the tooth. (Exodus 21:22-27)

This "eye for an eye" mentality might seem harsh to present day readers, but consider the following selection of laws from the Code of Hammurabi, a code that was seen to bring civility and order to society. Note too the ways that people of various social classes are valued differently.

3. If any one bring an accusation of any crime before the elders, and does not prove what he has charged, he shall, if it be a capital offense charged, be put to death.

6. If any one steal the property of a temple or of the court, he shall be put to death, and also the one who receives the stolen thing from him shall be put to death.

22. If any one is committing a robbery and is caught, then he shall be put to death.

25. If fire break out in a house, and some one who comes to put it out cast his eye upon the property of the owner of the house, and take the property of the master of the house, he shall be thrown into that self-same fire.

195. If a son strike his father, his hands shall be hewn off.

196. If a man put out the eye of another man, his eye shall be put out.

197. If he break another man's bone, his bone shall be broken.

198. If he put out the eye of a freed man, or break the bone of a freed man, he shall pay one gold mina.

199. If he put out the eye of a man's slave, or break the bone of a man's slave, he shall pay one-half of its value.

200. If a man knock out the teeth of his equal, his teeth shall be knocked out.

201. If he knock out the teeth of a freed man, he shall pay one-third of a gold mina.

Source: Code of Hammurabi

Notice the emphasis on body parts in these texts. Sometimes an offense can result in the loss of a body part. Other times offenses can be resolved by payment. Which of these seem inequitable to you?

Can you imagine a society wherein these laws might make more sense?

The Symbolism of Serpents

While the most well-known serpent in the Bible might be in Genesis 3, consider this fascinating story in Numbers 21:4-9:

> [4] Then they set out from Mount Hor by the way of the Red Sea (or Sea of Reeds), to go around the land of Edom; and the people became impatient because of the journey. [5] The people spoke against God and Moses, "Why have you brought us up out of Egypt to die in the wilderness? For there is no food (or bread) and no water, and we loathe this miserable food."
>
> [6] The Lord sent fiery serpents among the people and they bit the people, so that many people of Israel died. [7] So the people came to Moses and said, "We have sinned, because we have spoken against the Lord and you; intercede with the Lord, that He may remove the serpents from us." And Moses interceded for the people. [8] Then the Lord said to Moses, "Make a fiery serpent, and set it on a standard (or pole); and it shall come about, that everyone who is bitten, when he looks at it, he will live." [9] And Moses made a bronze serpent and set it on the standard (or pole); and it came about, that if a serpent bit any man, when he looked to the bronze serpent, he lived.

In Hebrew the word for serpents is *seraphim*. How does the symbol of a serpent function in this story? Is this symbol good, evil, neutral? As you consider this question, read Isaiah 6:1-3:

[1] In the year that King Uzziah died, I saw the Lord sitting on a throne, high and lofty; and the hem of his robe filled the temple. [2] Seraphs were in attendance above him; each had six wings: with two they covered their faces, and with two they covered their feet, and with two they flew. [3] And one called to another and said:

"Holy, holy, holy is the Lord of hosts;
the whole earth is full of his glory."

For more on this complicated symbol, read how this story is followed up in 2 Kings 18, or how it is used in the New Testament (John 3:15).

Levirate Marriage

One of the most important elements of ancient life was clan security and longevity. Many of the legal instructions for family life were meant to secure the power and wealth of the eldest son from generation to generation. Maintaining ongoing progeny in a dangerous world was paramount. Moreover, God's blessing to Abraham hinged on progeny. So having many sons and many grandsons was a religious mandate as well as a way to preserve to long-term health of one's clan. Knowing this will help us better understand legal requirements like "levirate marriage."

[5] When brothers reside together, and one of them dies and has no son, the wife of the deceased shall not be married outside the family to a stranger. Her husband's brother shall go in to her, taking her in marriage, and performing the duty of a husband's brother to her, [6] and the firstborn whom she bears shall succeed to the name of the deceased brother, so that his name may not be blotted out of Israel. [7] But if the man has no desire to marry his brother's widow, then his brother's widow shall go up to the elders at the gate and say, "My husband's brother refuses to perpetuate his brother's name in Israel; he will not perform the duty of a husband's brother to me." [8] Then the elders of his town shall summon him and speak to him. If he persists, saying, "I have no desire to marry her," [9] then his brother's wife shall go up to him in the presence of the elders, pull his sandal off his foot, spit in his face, and declare, "This is what is done to the man who does not build up his brother's house." [10] Throughout Israel his family shall be known as "the house of him whose sandal was pulled off." (Deuteronomy 25:5-10)

The law of levirate marriage goes like this: when a man dies without children, his brother is to marry the dead man's wife and have children in the name of the dead man so that there are heirs to inherit the family property. Crucially important here is that the biological father is not the "real" father. Rather the deceased brother functioned legally as the "real" father in this case so that his wealth could be legally passed to the next generation. This is among the most important sexual ethics in the Hebrew Bible. It will seem bizarre to modern ears, but this should remind us that Israel's legal instructions invite us to better understand an ancient and bygone culture. While we may not be able to appreciate all of their symbols, we may have a better understanding of our own symbols having read Leviticus.

Questions for Group Discussion

1. What do we learn about the personality of the Israelite God in the Pentateuch? Do any of the stories contained in these ancient text surprise you?
2. One of the most important verses of the Bible is Deuteronomy 6:4-9. Take a moment and read this text. What do we learn of God and Israel from this passage?
3. Read Numbers 27. What does the story of the daughters of Zelophehad suggest about the value and influence of women in the ancient world?

Questions for Reflection

1. How might you read Exodus differently if you were convinced that it was a historical narrative?

2. How might you read Exodus differently if you were convinced that it was purely fiction?

3. How might you read Exodus differently if you were convinced that it is a mixture of history and fiction?

6

The Israelites Tell Their Story: Interpretations of National Disasters

Summary and Learning Objectives

1. Israel's conquest and defense of the "promised land" tells of action-filled and often bloody episodes. Military leaders, judges, prophets, and kings are the key figures. Some of these stories form the foundation of Israel's institutionalized worship and political hopes for the future. After reading this chapter (alongside chapter 6 of Sumney's text), the reader should be able *to describe the era and reason for the writing of Joshua.*

2. After reading this chapter (alongside chapter 6 of Sumney's text), the reader should be able *to speak to at least three differences between ancient and modern ideas of conquest.*

3. After reading this chapter (alongside chapter 6 of Sumney's text), the reader should be able *to describe ancient Israel's relationship to polytheism.*

4. After reading this chapter (alongside chapter 6 of Sumney's text), the reader should be able *to name several key characters and their legacies in the Hebrew Bible, including Joshua, Deborah, Ruth, and David.*

5. After reading this chapter (alongside chapter 6 of Sumney's text), the reader should be able *to describe the era and reason for writing 1 and 2 Chronicles. The Reader should also be able to describe a few literary tendencies of the Chronicler.*

Key Terms

Asherah   Important Canaanite goddess, consort of Baal or of El.

Baal   Popular Canaanite god who ranked high in their pantheon. He was also the storm god.

Chronicler   The probably fourth-century author or authors of the books of 1 and 2 Chronicles. This group was also related to the authors of Ezra and Nehemiah.

City of Refuge A city established as a place to which those accused of murder could flee for protection until trial. If found not guilty they could remain under its protection.

Deuteronomistic history The telling of the story of the life of the nations of the Israelites from the perspective of the paradigm set out in Deuteronomy (that is, faithfulness brings blessing to the nation and unfaithfulness will bring defeat and disaster). The books of Joshua, Judges, 1 and 2 Samuel, and 1 and 2 Kings are all written from this perspective and are called the deuteronomistic histories.

Polytheism The worship of many gods.

Ruth Moabite widow of an Israelite who returns to Israelite territory with her mother-in-law, committing herself to the God of Israel. Through the system of levirate marriage, she marries Boaz. Her great-grandson is King David.

Satan A word that means opposer. This term evolves into the name of a personified evil in Second Temple Judaism.

Key Themes

- ▶ Many kings in the ancient world viewed military conquest and the mass killing of entire clans as a way to establish peace
- ▶ In a world of harsh consequences, both Israelites and later Jewish thinkers attempted to imagine alternatives to execution

- ▶ Later biblical authors and editors attempt to explain the unfaithfulness of Israel as the cause of political catastrophe
- ▶ When reading biblical stories, it is crucial to understand what motivates the main characters

Primary Text

Conquest

Joshua is among the most disturbing books of the Bible to modern sensibilities. We are repeatedly reminded that the stories told of the ancient Israelites are foreign in time, place, and culture to our own. For example:

36 Then Joshua went up with all Israel from Eglon to Hebron; they assaulted it, 37 and took it, and struck it with the edge of the sword, and its king and its towns, and every person in it; he left no one remaining, just as he had done to Eglon, and utterly destroyed it with every person in it.

38 Then Joshua, with all Israel, turned back to Debir and assaulted it, 39 and he took it with its king and all its towns; they struck them with the edge of the sword, and utterly destroyed every person in it; he left no one remaining, just as he had done to Hebron, and, as he had done to Libnah and its king, so he did to Debir and its king.

40 So Joshua defeated the whole land, the hill country and the Negeb and the lowland and the slopes, and all their kings; he left no one remaining, but utterly destroyed all that breathed, as the Lord God of Israel commanded. 41 And Joshua defeated them from Kadesh-barnea to Gaza, and all

the country of Goshen, as far as Gibeon. [42] Joshua took all these kings and their land at one time, because the Lord God of Israel fought for Israel. [43] Then Joshua returned, and all Israel with him, to the camp at Gilgal. (Joshua 10:36-43)

This story gives us a brief glimpse into how different our ideas of religion are from the ancient world. When we imagine war, we are repulsed by any religious elements of violence. But in the ancient world, many believed that human violence was justified only when it was divinely endorsed. Furthermore, our steadfast condemnation of genocide would have seemed strange to the world of the ancient Israelites. They did not have the category of "genocide" and—as repulsive as it will be to us—many believed that the mass killings of entire clans was praiseworthy. With this in mind, consider this artifact from Egypt. The Merneptah Stele is a large granite slab that showcases an inscription from the reign of Pharaoh Merneptah (1212–1202 B.C.E.). This inscription has interested biblical scholars because it probably contains the name "Israel." If so, the Merneptah Stele is among our oldest (many believe *the* oldest) historical records for the existence of Israel as a people. Here is an excerpt:

> The princes are prostrate, saying: "Peace" (shalama);
> No one is raising his head among the Nine Bows;
> Now the Tehenu (Libya) has come to ruin;
> Hatti is pacified;
> The Canaan has been plundered into every sort of woe;
> Ashkelon has been overcome;
> Gezer has been captured;
> Yano'am is made nonexistent;

> Israel is laid waste and his seed is not (or *his offspring is no more*);
> Hurru is become a widow because of Egypt.

Source: K. A. Kitchen, *Ramesside Inscriptions, Historical and Biographical,* 8 vols., (Oxford: Blackwell, 1975–1990), 4:12–19.

Notice here that the voice of the Pharaoh boasts about wiping out entire clans of people. This, of course, would not be publicized by political leaders in modern society. We would call such an act "genocide" and the leader in question would be tried for war crimes. But, to many in the ancient world, such reports were considered praiseworthy and spoke of a king's power and ability to bring peace to his lands. As modern readers we find such reports to be deeply troubling, and rightly so.

But also notice that with such bragging comes exaggeration. Indeed, we know that Israel was not "laid waste" completely. Indeed the "seed" of Abraham continued even after multiple exiles.

The Moabite Stone (also called the Stele of Mesha) is another such account. It celebrates the exploits of the king of Moab, mentioning victories over kings of Israel. Compare what he says about his nation's defeats and his victories.

> I (am) Mesha, son of Chemosh [. . .] king of Moab . . . who made this high place for Chemosh om Qarhoh [. . .] because he saved me from all the kings and caused me to triumph over all my adversaries. As for Omri, king of Israel, he humbled Moab many years, for Chemosh was angry at his land. And his son (Ahab) followed him and he also said, "I will humble Moab." In my time he spoke (thus), but I have triumphed over him and over his house, while Israel has perished forever. (lines 1–9)

Source: W. F. Albright, trans., *Ancient Near Eastern Texts Relating to the Old Testament*, 2nd ed., ed. James B. Pritchard (Princeton: Princeton University Press, 1955), 320, revised.

Given how conquest and the extermination of entire clans were understood in the ancient world, how might have the ancient Israelites read a book like Joshua differently than modern readers?

Cities of Refuge

Consider this passage from Joshua chapter 20:

[1] Then the Lord spoke to Joshua, saying, [2] "Say to the Israelites, 'Appoint the cities of refuge, of which I spoke to you through Moses, [3] so that anyone who kills a person without intent or by mistake may flee there; they shall be for you a refuge from the avenger of blood. [4] The slayer shall flee to one of these cities and shall stand at the entrance of the gate of the city, and explain the case to the elders of that city; then the fugitive shall be taken into the city, and given a place, and shall remain with them. [5] And if the avenger of blood is in pursuit, they shall not give up the slayer, because the neighbor was killed by mistake, there having been no enmity between them before. [6] The slayer shall remain in that city until there is a trial before the congregation, until the death of the one who is high priest at the time: then the slayer may return home, to the town in which the deed was done.' "

[7] So they set apart Kedesh in Galilee in the hill country of Naphtali, and Shechem in the hill country of Ephraim, and Kiriath-arba (that is, Hebron) in the hill country of Judah. [8] And beyond the Jordan east of Jericho, they appointed Bezer in the wilderness on the tableland, from the tribe of Reuben, and Ramoth in Gilead, from the tribe of Gad, and Golan in Bashan, from the tribe of Manasseh. [9] These were the cities designated for all the Israelites, and for the aliens residing among them, that anyone who killed a person without intent could flee there, so as not to die by the hand of the avenger of blood, until there was a trial before the congregation. (Joshua 20:1-9)

The Talmud (Makkot 11) reveals a discussion of the cities of refuge:

II. The penalty of exile (banishment) (2:1-8); A. Those who are sent into exile: These are the ones who go into exile (mainly: involuntary manslaughter). He who throws a stone into the public domain and committed homicide—lo, this one goes into exile. . . B Where do they go into exile? To the cities of refuge. Yose b. R. Judah: The procedure by which a person flees to a city of refuge and is tried.

Source: Jacob Neusner, trans. and ed., *The Talmud of the Land of Israel*, Vol. 31: Sanhedrin and Makkot (Chicago: University of Chicago Press, 1984, 396–97.

The rabbis who discuss these legal instructions centuries after the writing of Joshua are deeply concerned that alternatives to execution are found wherever possible. While every action that results in death (even accidental) must come with a consequence, the rabbis knew that no solution was perfect. So we hear a continued discussion about how to best implement such legal instructions.

Women in Judges

The ancient world was a very dangerous place for women (as is still true in many parts of today's world). This fact makes the story of Deborah from the book of Judges even more remarkable:

[1] The Israelites again did what was evil in the sight of the Lord, after Ehud died. [2] So the Lord sold them into the hand of King Jabin of Canaan, who reigned in Hazor; the commander of his army was Sisera, who lived in Harosheth-ha-goiim. [3] Then the Israelites cried out to the Lord for help; for he had nine hundred chariots of iron, and had oppressed the Israelites cruelly twenty years.

[4] At that time Deborah, a prophetess, wife of Lappidoth, was judging Israel. [5] She used to sit under the palm of Deborah between Ramah and Bethel in the hill country of Ephraim; and the Israelites came up to her for judgment. [6] She sent and summoned Barak son of Abinoam from Kedesh in Naphtali, and said to him, "The Lord, the God of Israel, commands you, 'Go, take position at Mount Tabor, bringing ten thousand from the tribe of Naphtali and the tribe of Zebulun. [7] I will draw out Sisera, the general of Jabin's army, to meet you by the Wadi Kishon with his chariots and his troops; and I will give him into your hand.'" [8] Barak said to her, "If you will go with me, I will go; but if you will not go with me, I will not go." [9] And she said, "I will surely go with you; nevertheless, the road on which you are going will not lead to your glory, for the Lord will sell Sisera into the hand of a woman." Then Deborah got up and went with Barak to Kedesh.

[10] Barak summoned Zebulun and Naphtali to Kedesh; and ten thousand warriors went up behind him; and Deborah went up with him. [11] Now Heber the Kenite had separated from the other Kenites, that is, the descendants of Hobab the father-in-law of Moses, and had encamped as far away as Elon-bezaanannim, which is near Kedesh. [12] When Sisera was told that Barak son of Abinoam had gone up to Mount Tabor, [13] Sisera called out all his chariots, nine hundred chariots of iron, and all the troops who were with him, from Harosheth-ha-goiim to the Wadi Kishon. [14] Then Deborah said to Barak, "Up! For this is the day on which the Lord has given Sisera into your hand. The Lord is indeed going out before you." So Barak went down from Mount Tabor with ten thousand warriors following him. [15] And the Lord threw Sisera and all his chariots and all his army into a panic before Barak; Sisera got down from his chariot and fled away on foot, [16] while Barak pursued the chariots and the army to Harosheth-ha-goiim. All the army of Sisera fell by the sword; no one was left.

[17] Now Sisera had fled away on foot to the tent of Jael wife of Heber the Kenite; for there was peace between King Jabin of Hazor and the clan of Heber the Kenite. [18] Jael came out to meet Sisera, and said to him, "Turn aside, my lord, turn aside to me; have no fear." So he turned aside to her into the tent, and she covered him with a rug. [19] Then he said to her, "Please give me a little water to drink; for I am thirsty." So she opened a skin of milk and gave him a drink and covered him. [20] He said to her,

"Stand at the entrance of the tent, and if anybody comes and asks you, 'Is anyone here?' say, 'No.' " [21] But Jael wife of Heber took a tent peg, and took a hammer in her hand, and went softly to him and drove the peg into his temple, until it went down into the ground—he was lying fast asleep from weariness—and he died. [22] Then, as Barak came in pursuit of Sisera, Jael went out to meet him, and said to him, "Come, and I will show you the man whom you are seeking." So he went into her tent; and there was Sisera lying dead, with the tent peg in his temple. [23] So on that day God subdued King Jabin of Canaan before the Israelites. [24] Then the hand of the Israelites bore harder and harder on King Jabin of Canaan, until they destroyed King Jabin of Canaan. (Judges 4:1-24)

Compare the female characters in the above story to the nameless woman who is violently murdered in Judges 19:

[1] In those days, when there was no king in Israel, a certain Levite, residing in the remote parts of the hill country of Ephraim, took to himself a concubine from Bethlehem in Judah. [2] But his concubine became angry with him, and she went away from him to her father's house at Bethlehem in Judah, and was there some four months. [3] Then her husband set out after her, to speak tenderly to her and bring her back. He had with him his servant and a couple of donkeys. When he reached her father's house, the girl's father saw him and came with joy to meet him. [4] His father-in-law, the girl's father, made him stay, and he remained with him three days; so they ate and drank, and he stayed there. [5] On the fourth day they got up early in the morning, and he prepared to go; but the girl's father said to his son-in-law, "Fortify yourself with a bit of food, and after that you may go." [6] So the two men sat and ate and drank together; and the girl's father said to the man, "Why not spend the night and enjoy yourself?" [7] When the man got up to go, his father-in-law kept urging him until he spent the night there again. [8] On the fifth day he got up early in the morning to leave; and the girl's father said, "Fortify yourself." So they lingered until the day declined, and the two of them ate and drank. [9] When the man with his concubine and his servant got up to leave, his father-in-law, the girl's father, said to him, "Look, the day has worn on until it is almost evening. Spend the night. See, the day has drawn to a close. Spend the night here and enjoy yourself. Tomorrow you can get up early in the morning for your journey, and go home." [10] But the man would not spend the night; he got up and departed, and arrived opposite Jebus (that is, Jerusalem). He had with him a couple of saddled donkeys, and his concubine was with him. [11] When they were near Jebus, the day was far spent, and the servant said to his master, "Come now, let us turn aside to this city of the Jebusites, and spend the night in it." [12] But his master said to him, "We will not turn aside into a city of foreigners, who do not belong to the people of Israel; but we will continue on to Gibeah."

¹³ Then he said to his servant, "Come, let us try to reach one of these places, and spend the night at Gibeah or at Ramah." ¹⁴ So they passed on and went their way; and the sun went down on them near Gibeah, which belongs to Benjamin. ¹⁵ They turned aside there, to go in and spend the night at Gibeah. He went in and sat down in the open square of the city, but no one took them in to spend the night.

¹⁶ Then at evening there was an old man coming from his work in the field. The man was from the hill country of Ephraim, and he was residing in Gibeah. (The people of the place were Benjaminites.) ¹⁷ When the old man looked up and saw the wayfarer in the open square of the city, he said, "Where are you going and where do you come from?" ¹⁸ He answered him, "We are passing from Bethlehem in Judah to the remote parts of the hill country of Ephraim, from which I come. I went to Bethlehem in Judah; and I am going to my home. Nobody has offered to take me in. ¹⁹ We your servants have straw and fodder for our donkeys, with bread and wine for me and the woman and the young man along with us. We need nothing more." ²⁰ The old man said, "Peace be to you. I will care for all your wants; only do not spend the night in the square." ²¹ So he brought him into his house, and fed the donkeys; they washed their feet, and ate and drank. (Judges 19:1-21)

Both of these stories portray a violent world wherein social power (or lack thereof) could mean the difference between life and death. What do we learn of the various roles of women in these stories?

Plotting Ruth's Motivations

One of the crucial questions of literary analysis is this: *What motivates the main character in this story?* There are several ways to answer this, but this question is generally related to a primary problem in the life of the main character. The vast majority of stories attempt to solve a problem. With this in mind consider the first paragraphs of the book of Ruth:

¹ In the days when the judges ruled, there was a famine in the land, and a certain man of Bethlehem in Judah went to live in the country of Moab, he and his wife and two sons. ² The name of the man was Elimelech and the name of his wife Naomi, and the names of his two sons were Mahlon and Chilion; they were Ephrathites from Bethlehem in Judah. They went into the country of Moab and remained there. ³ But Elimelech, the husband of Naomi, died, and she was left with her two sons. ⁴ These took Moabite wives; the name of the one was Orpah and the name of the other Ruth. When they had lived there about ten years, ⁵ both Mahlon and Chilion also died, so that the woman was left without her two sons and her husband.

⁶ Then she started to return with her daughters-in-law from the country of Moab, for she had heard in the country of Moab that the Lord had considered his people and given them food. ⁷ So she set out from the place where she had been living, she and her two daughters-in-law, and they went on their way to go back to the land of Judah. ⁸ But Naomi said to her two daughters-in-law, "Go back each of you to your mother's house. May the Lord deal kindly with you, as you have dealt with the

dead and with me. [9] The Lord grant that you may find security, each of you in the house of your husband." Then she kissed them, and they wept aloud. [10] They said to her, "No, we will return with you to your people." [11] But Naomi said, "Turn back, my daughters, why will you go with me? Do I still have sons in my womb that they may become your husbands? [12] Turn back, my daughters, go your way, for I am too old to have a husband. Even if I thought there was hope for me, even if I should have a husband tonight and bear sons, [13] would you then wait until they were grown? Would you then refrain from marrying? No, my daughters, it has been far more bitter for me than for you, because the hand of the Lord has turned against me." [14] Then they wept aloud again. Orpah kissed her mother-in-law, but Ruth clung to her. (Ruth 1:1-14)

Who is Ruth? What country is she from? What is Ruth's fundamental problem?

Siloam Inscription

When Israel fell to the Assyrians, Judah was also threatened. This inscription tells of the preparations for a siege. It is found in a tunnel brings that water into Jerusalem so that they can better withstand a siege. According to 2 Kings 20:20, King Hezekiah brought water to the city through a conduit. Many archeologists identify the tunnel talked about in this inscription with Hezekiah's waterworks project. So it is often called Hezekiah's tunnel. The Siloam inscription reads:

And this was the manner in which they bored through; while yet . . . the pick, each toward the other diggers, and while yet there were four and a half feet to be bored [through, there was hear]d the voice of each calling the other group of diggers, for there was a split in the rock on the right hand . . . And on the day they bored through the miners struck, each to meet the other diggers, pick upon pick; and the waters flowed from the source to the pool for 1,800 feet; and the height of the rock above the head of the miners (when they were in the tunnel) was 1,500 feet.

Source: G. A. Cooke, *A Text-book of North-Semitic Inscriptions* (Oxford: Clarendon, 1903.), revised.

The Chronicler as Revisionist

The author or authors of the books related to Chronicles has a unique take on the Israelite monarchies. First and Second Chronicles shape their story of Israelite kings highlights the topic of faithfulness (or lack thereof) in the legacy of each king. Even more than the deuteronomistic historians, the Chronicler emphasizes the pattern Deuteronomy sets out for Israel's national life: the nation's and king's faithfulness brings blessings from God, worship of other gods brings disaster. When this pattern breaks down in the deuteronomistic histories, Chronicles changes the account so that disaster comes on a king only as a result of unfaithfulness. Beyond this general revisionism, consider the difference between these two accounts of the Davidic Covenant:

¹² When your days are fulfilled and you lie down with your ancestors, I will raise up your offspring after you, who shall come forth from your body, and I will establish his kingdom. ¹³ He shall build a house for my name, and I will establish the throne of his kingdom forever. ¹⁴ I will be a father to him, and he shall be a son to me. When he commits iniquity, I will punish him with a rod such as mortals use, with blows inflicted by human beings. (2 Samuel 7:12-14)

¹¹ When your days are fulfilled to go to be with your ancestors, I will raise up your offspring after you, one of your own sons, and I will establish his kingdom. ¹² He shall build a house for me, and I will establish his throne forever. ¹³ I will be a father to him, and he shall be a son to me. I will not take my steadfast love from him, as I took it from him who was before you, ¹⁴ but I will confirm him in my house and in my kingdom forever, and his throne shall be established forever. (1 Chronicles 17:11-14)

In the Lord's promise to David, this covenant looks forward to Solomon's complicated legacy: beloved by God, but not without personal failure. Why would the Chronicler (writing much later than 2 Samuel) leave out the details of Solomon's failures?

Consider also the stark difference in the accounts of David's census:

¹ Satan stood up against Israel, and incited David to count the people of Israel. ² So David said to Joab and the commanders of the army, "Go, number Israel, from Beer-sheba to Dan, and bring me a report, so that I may know their number." ³ But Joab said, "May the Lord increase the number of his people a hundredfold! Are they not, my lord the king, all of them my lord's servants? Why then should my lord require this? Why should he bring guilt on Israel?" (1 Chronicles 21:1-3)

¹ Again the anger of the Lord was kindled against Israel, and he incited David against them, saying, "Go, count the people of Israel and Judah." ² So the king said to Joab and the commanders of the army, who were with him, "Go through all the tribes of Israel, from Dan to Beer-sheba, and take a census of the people, so that I may know how many there are." ³ But Joab said to the king, "May the Lord your God increase the number of the people a hundredfold, while the eyes of my lord the king can still see it! But why does my lord the king want to do this?" (2 Samuel 24:1-3)

What motivates David to take this census according to 2 Samuel 24? What motivates David to take this census according to 1 Chronicles 21? Why would the Chronicler (writing in the fourth century B.C.E.) introduce the character of "Satan" into this narrative? What sort of ideological or theological shift does this suggest?

Questions for Group Discussion

1. What is the relationship between God and politics in ancient Israelite thought?
2. What are a few differences between modern and ancient understandings of warfare?
3. What are the varying social positions occupied by the women discussed in this section?

Questions for Reflection

1. Would it be appropriate to call the books of Chronicles examples of revisionist history?

2. In what ways do such violent stories function as sacred texts in the modern world?

7

"Thus Says the Lord": Israel's Prophetic Tradition

Summary and Learning Objectives

1. The prophets of the Hebrew Bible are voices that speak out about the political situations of their days as well as about the future. These voices give us insights into Israel's political commentary and hopes for renewal, judgment, and ultimate peace.

2. After reading this chapter (alongside chapter 7 of Sumney's text), the reader should be able *to identify at least three keys issues of social justice and ethics emphasized by the ancient Hebrew prophets.*

3. After reading this chapter (alongside chapter 7 of Sumney's text), the reader should be able *to explain why judgment is an important part of Hebrew prophecy.*

4. After reading this chapter (alongside chapter 7 of Sumney's text), the reader should be able *to identify a few historic events that are important for shaping the imaginations of Hebrew prophecy.*

5. After reading this chapter (alongside chapter 7 of Sumney's text), the reader should be able *to describe some of the symbols of Hebrew prophecy (both in actions and in dreams).*

Key Terms

Amos   Eighth-century Israelite prophet. He insisted that socioeconomic justice and personal morality must accompany worship of God.

Cyrus   Ruler of the Persian empire (539–530 B.C.E.) who allows the Jadeites (the remaining Israelites) to return to their ancestral land (Judah). Isaiah calls him God's messiah, or anointed one (Isaiah 45:1-3).

Day of the Lord   Originally it was a phrase prophets used to speak of the time when God would act on the behalf of the Israelites to bring them victory. Later prophets reverse its meaning to warn of the time when God would act against Israel and Judah because of their unfaithfulness to God.

Ezekiel Sixth-century prophet who was taken to Babylon in the first wave of exiles from Jerusalem in 597 B.C.E. There he has dramatic visions about the presence of God moving to be with the exiles. These visions contributed much to the development of apocalyptic thought and imagery.

Messiah Anointed one. Various people throughout the Hebrew Bible were anointed, a way of appointing someone to perform specific tasks.

Micah Eighth-century Israelite prophet who emphasized the importance of social justice. He argued that God will not accept the worship of people who treat others unjustly.

Key Themes

▶ With political power and wealth comes responsibility for the poor and disenfranchised

▶ Historical and political commentary is often shaped by historic "types"

▶ Prophets will sometimes act out their symbols, rather than just speak them

Primary Text

Condemnation on the Abuses of Power

One of the major themes of the prophets is the Lord's anger at those who abuse their power and exploit the powerless. Read through the following passage in Amos and identify the particular abuses of power that are condemned.

⁶ Thus says the Lord: For three transgressions of Israel, and for four, I will not revoke the punishment; because they sell the righteous for silver, and the needy for a pair of sandals—⁷ they who trample the head of the poor into the dust of the earth, and push the afflicted out of the way; father and son go in to the same girl, so that my holy name is profaned; ⁸ they lay themselves down beside every altar on garments taken in pledge; and in the house of their God they drink wine bought with fines they imposed.

⁹ Yet I destroyed the Amorite before them, whose height was like the height of cedars, and who was as strong as oaks; I destroyed his fruit above, and his roots beneath. ¹⁰ Also I brought you up out of the land of Egypt, and led you forty years in the wilderness, to possess the land of the Amorite. ¹¹ And I raised up some of your children to be prophets and some of your youths to be nazirites. Is it not indeed so, O people of Israel? says the Lord. ¹² But you made the nazirites drink wine, and commanded the prophets, saying, "You shall not prophesy." ¹³ So, I will press you down in your place, just as a cart presses down when it is full of sheaves. ¹⁴ Flight shall perish from the swift, and the strong shall not retain their strength, nor shall the mighty save their lives; ¹⁵ those who handle the bow shall not stand, and those who are swift of foot shall not save themselves, nor shall those who ride horses save their lives; ¹⁶ and those who are stout of heart among the mighty shall flee away naked in that day, says the Lord. (Amos 2:6-16)

Consider also the abuses of wealth that are condemned in Micah. Look for the various symbols for wealth in this passage:

⁶ "With what shall I come before the Lord, and bow myself before God on high? Shall I come before him with burnt offerings, with calves a year old? ⁷ Will the Lord be pleased with thousands of rams, with ten thousands of rivers of oil? Shall I give my firstborn for my transgression, the fruit of my body for the sin of my soul?" ⁸ He has told you, O mortal, what is good; and what does the Lord require of you but to do justice, and to love kindness, and to walk humbly with your God?

⁹ The voice of the Lord cries to the city (it is sound wisdom to fear your name): Hear, O tribe and assembly of the city! ¹⁰ Can I forget the treasures of wickedness in the house of the wicked, and the scant measure that is accursed? ¹¹ Can I tolerate wicked scales and a bag of dishonest weights? ¹² Your wealthy are full of violence; your inhabitants speak lies, with tongues of deceit in their mouths. ¹³ Therefore I have begun to strike you down, making you desolate because of your sins. ¹⁴ You shall eat, but not be satisfied, and there shall be a gnawing hunger within you; you shall put away, but not save, and what you save, I will hand over to the sword. ¹⁵ You shall sow, but not reap; you shall tread olives, but not anoint yourselves with oil; you shall tread grapes, but not drink wine. ¹⁶ For you have kept the statutes of Omri and all the works of the house of Ahab, and you have followed their counsels. Therefore I will make you a desolation, and your inhabitants an object of hissing; so you shall bear the scorn of my people. (Micah 6:6-16)

The gods of other peoples also called kings to work for justice. A letter from Mari (1800–1700 B.C.E.) from a court official to the king contains the following:

> The *apilum* prophet of Addu, God of Halab, said to me: "Am I not Addu, God of Halab, who raised you . . . who helped you gain your father's throne? I never ask too much of you. Respond to the appeals of your people when they experience injustice and give them a just verdict.
>
> You are to do what I ask and what I write to you to do. You will obey my word and keep watch over this land continually.

Source: A.2925 from V. H. Matthews and D. C. Benjamin, "Archives Royales de Mari, Textes Cuneiforms" in *Old Testament Parallels: Laws and Stories from the Ancient Near East* (Mahwah, New Jersey: Paulist Press, 1991), 109–110, revised.

Judgment and Wrath

To many modern readers the notion of a "God of Judgment" is disturbing. But to many ancient Israelite sensibilities the idea of God as divine judge was comforting. Many ancient Israelites saw their sons slaughtered in warfare and their daughters carried off as slaves. Even worse, corrupt leaders both inside and outside Israel were blind to the needs of the poorest among them. It was a world (much like ours) where powerful but corrupt men went unpunished. In this world, the hope that God would soon come to judge the wicked and find them guilty was comforting. They hoped that the innocent would be judged and found innocent (thus justice would be served). This day of judgment was often called "The Day of the Lord." Consider this description from Ezekiel 13:1-16:

[1] The word of the Lord came to me: [2] Mortal, prophesy against the prophets of Israel who are prophesying; say to those who prophesy out of their own imagination: "Hear the word of the Lord!" [3] Thus says the Lord God, Alas for the senseless prophets who follow their own spirit, and have seen nothing! [4] Your prophets have been like jackals among ruins, O Israel. [5] You have not gone up into the breaches, or repaired a wall for the house of Israel, so that it might stand in battle on the day of the Lord. [6] They have envisioned falsehood and lying divination; they say, "Says the Lord," when the Lord has not sent them, and yet they wait for the fulfillment of their word! [7] Have you not seen a false vision or uttered a lying divination, when you have said, "Says the Lord," even though I did not speak? [8] Therefore thus says the Lord God: Because you have uttered falsehood and envisioned lies, I am against you, says the Lord God. [9] My hand will be against the prophets who see false visions and utter lying divinations; they shall not be in the council of my people, nor be enrolled in the register of the house of Israel, nor shall they enter the land of Israel; and you shall know that I am the Lord God.

[10] Because, in truth, because they have misled my people, saying, "Peace," when there is no peace; and because, when the people build a wall, these prophets smear whitewash on it. [11] Say to those who smear whitewash on it that it shall fall. There will be a deluge of rain, great hailstones will fall, and a stormy wind will break out. [12] When the wall falls, will it not be said to you, "Where is the whitewash you smeared on it?" [13] Therefore thus says the Lord God: In my wrath I will make a stormy wind break out, and in my anger there shall be a deluge of rain, and hailstones in wrath to destroy it. [14] I will break down the wall that you have smeared with whitewash, and bring it to the ground, so that its foundation will be laid bare; when it falls, you shall perish within it; and you shall know that I am the Lord. [15] Thus I will spend my wrath upon the wall, and upon those who have smeared it with whitewash; and I will say to you, The wall is no more, nor those who smeared it—[16] the prophets of Israel who prophesied concerning Jerusalem and saw visions of peace for it, when there was no peace, says the Lord God.

In this oracle, Ezekiel warns the people of Israel that some of their prophets have not prepared them for the Day of the Lord. Ezekiel reminds them that the Day of the Lord will be terrible for prophets who have offered false messages of comfort.

Historic Types

Sometimes the Hebrew prophets imaginatively draw from great moments in Israel's history to explain types of historic events. Many believed that foreign kings of the present would act like the foreign kings of the past. Many believed that the Lord would act again in the present as the Lord acted in the past. Thus, a historic "type" was used to explain political events. When a foreign king acted like the iconic Pharaoh of the Egyptian exile, the prophets would recognize that type of king right away and remind the people of Israel what they could expect from their God. It is almost as if these prophets were saying: "our God is the type of god who punishes these types of kings!" Many kings in Israel's prophecies were praised if they looked like David or Solomon types. Compare this story about Solomon to Isaiah's hopes for a wise king:

> 16 Later, two women who were prostitutes came to the king and stood before him. 17 The one woman said, "Please, my lord, this woman and I live in the same house; and I gave birth while she was in the house. 18 Then on the third day after I gave birth, this woman also gave birth. We were together; there was no one else with us in the house, only the two of us were in the house. 19 Then this woman's son died in the night, because she lay on him. 20 She got up in the middle of the night and took my son from beside me while your servant slept. She laid him at her breast, and laid her dead son at my breast. 21 When I rose in the morning to nurse my son, I saw that he was dead; but when I looked at him closely in the morning, clearly it was not the son I had borne." 22 But the other woman said, "No, the living son is mine, and the dead son is yours." The first said, "No, the dead son is yours, and the living son is mine." So they argued before the king. 23 Then the king said, "The one says, 'This is my son that is alive, and your son is dead'; while the other says, 'Not so! Your son is dead, and my son is the living one.'" 24 So the king said, "Bring me a sword," and they brought a sword before the king. 25 The king said, "Divide the living boy in two; then give half to the one, and half to the other." 26 But the woman whose son was alive said to the king—because compassion for her son burned within her—"Please, my lord, give her the living boy; certainly do not kill him!" The other said, "It shall be neither mine nor yours; divide it." 27 Then the king responded: "Give the first woman the living boy; do not kill him. She is his mother." 28 All Israel heard of the judgment that the king had rendered; and they stood in awe of the king, because they perceived that the wisdom of God was in him, to execute justice. (1 Kings 3:16-28)

Now read these passages from Isaiah chapters 9 and 11.

> 6 For a child has been born for us, a son given to us; authority rests upon his shoulders; and he is named Wonderful Counselor, Mighty God, Everlasting Father, Prince of Peace. 7 His authority shall grow continually, and there shall be endless peace for the throne of David and his kingdom. He will establish and uphold it with justice and with righteousness from this time onward and forevermore. The zeal of the Lord of hosts will do this. (Isaiah 9:6-7)

> 1 A shoot shall come out from the stump of Jesse, and a branch shall grow out of his roots. 2 The spirit of the Lord shall rest on him, the spirit of wisdom and understanding, the spirit of counsel and might, the spirit of knowledge and the fear of the Lord. 3 His delight shall be in the fear of the Lord. He shall not judge by what his eyes see, or decide by what his ears hear; 4 but with righteousness he shall judge the poor, and decide with equity for the meek of the earth; he shall strike the earth with the rod of his mouth, and with the breath

of his lips he shall kill the wicked. [5] Righteousness shall be the belt around his waist, and faithfulness the belt around his loins. (Isaiah 11:1-5)

What does Solomon have in common with the king mentioned in Isaiah?

The edict of the Persian king Cyrus allowing the Jewish exiles in Babylon to return to Jerusalem and rebuild the temple is quoted in 2 Chronicles 36:22-23; Ezra 1:1-4; and 6:3-5. The version of this decree in Ezra 1:1-4 reads:

> [1] In the first year of King Cyrus of Persia, in order that the word of the Lord by the mouth of Jeremiah might be accomplished, the Lord stirred up the spirit of King Cyrus of Persia so that he sent a herald throughout all his kingdom, and also in a [2] written edict declared: [3] Any of those among you who are of his people—may their God be with them! —are now permitted to go up to Jerusalem in Judah, and rebuild the house of the Lord, the God of Israel—he is the God who is in Jerusalem; [4] and let all survivors, in whatever place they reside, be assisted by the people of their place with silver and gold, with goods and with animals, besides freewill offerings for the house of God in Jerusalem."

Because of this decree by this gentile (that is, non-Jewish) king, he is considered a type of "anointed one" or "messiah" according to Isaiah 45:1-7:

> [1] Thus says the Lord to his anointed, to Cyrus, whose right hand I have grasped to subdue nations before him and strip kings of their robes, to open doors before

him—and the gates shall not be closed: [2] I will go before you and level the mountains, I will break in pieces the doors of bronze and cut through the bars of iron, [3] I will give you the treasures of darkness and riches hidden in secret places, so that you may know that it is I, the Lord, the God of Israel, who call you by your name. [4] For the sake of my servant Jacob, and Israel my chosen, I call you by your name, I surname you, though you do not know me.

> [5] I am the Lord, and there is no other; besides me there is no god. I arm you, though you do not know me, [6] so that they may know, from the rising of the sun and from the west, that there is no one besides me; I am the Lord, and there is no other. [7] I form light and create darkness, I make weal and create woe; I the Lord do all these things.

Previous to Cyrus, only Hebrew kings and prophets were considered to be "anointed" by God. But the example of Cyrus reminds us that historic types can be applied in new and unprecedented ways.

Prophetic Action

It might be tempting to think of Hebrew prophecy as simply oracles or speeches. But these prophets would sometimes act out their prophecies. For example, Isaiah was told to walk around naked for three years to symbolize the shame of Egypt. Consider Isaiah 20:1-4:

> [1] In the year that the commander-in-chief, who was sent by King Sargon of Assyria, came to Ashdod and fought against it and took it—[2] at that time the Lord had spoken

to Isaiah son of Amoz, saying, "Go, and loose the sackcloth from your loins and take your sandals off your feet," and he had done so, walking naked and barefoot. [3] Then the Lord said, "Just as my servant Isaiah has walked naked and barefoot for three years as a sign and a portent against Egypt and Ethiopia, [4] so shall the king of Assyria lead away the Egyptians as captives and the Ethiopians as exiles, both the young and the old, naked and barefoot, with buttocks uncovered, to the shame of Egypt.

Or consider this prophetic action by Ezekiel 4:4-15:

[4] Then lie on your left side, and place the punishment of the house of Israel upon it; you shall bear their punishment for the number of the days that you lie there. [5] For I assign to you a number of days, three hundred ninety days, equal to the number of the years of their punishment; and so you shall bear the punishment of the house of Israel. [6] When you have completed these, you shall lie down a second time, but on your right side, and bear the punishment of the house of Judah; forty days I assign you, one day for each year. [7] You shall set your face toward the siege of Jerusalem, and with your arm bared you shall prophesy against it. [8] See, I am putting cords on you so that you cannot turn from one side to the other until you have completed the days of your siege.

[9] And you, take wheat and barley, beans and lentils, millet and spelt; put them into one vessel, and make bread for yourself. During the number of days that you lie on your side, three hundred ninety days, you shall eat it. [10] The food that you eat shall be twenty shekels a day by weight; at fixed times you shall eat it. [11] And you shall drink water by measure, one-sixth of a hin; at fixed times you shall drink. [12] You shall eat it as a barley-cake, baking it in their sight on human dung. [13] The Lord said, "Thus shall the people of Israel eat their bread, unclean, among the nations to which I will drive them." [14] Then I said, "Ah Lord God! I have never defiled myself; from my youth up until now I have never eaten what died of itself or was torn by animals, nor has carrion flesh come into my mouth." [15] Then he said to me, "See, I will let you have cow's dung instead of human dung, on which you may prepare your bread."

As seen here, each of these actions symbolized a political statement in the life of Ezekiel. What are some of the symbols and what do they mean according to this passage?

Sometimes prophets were relatively inactive when they received a vision. It was not uncommon for prophets in the ancient world to convey and interpret a dream that they had. Consider this "night vision" from Zechariah:

[8] In the night I saw a man riding on a red horse! He was standing among the myrtle trees in the glen; and behind him were red, sorrel, and white horses. [9] Then I said, "What are these, my lord?" The angel who talked with me said to me, "I will show you what they are." [10] So the man who was standing among the myrtle trees answered, "They are those whom the Lord has sent

to patrol the earth." [11] Then they spoke to the angel of the Lord who was standing among the myrtle trees, "We have patrolled the earth, and lo, the whole earth remains at peace." [12] Then the angel of the Lord said, "O Lord of hosts, how long will you withhold mercy from Jerusalem and the cities of Judah, with which you have been angry these seventy years?" [13] Then the Lord replied with gracious and comforting words to the angel who talked with me. [14] So the angel who talked with me said to me, Proclaim this message: Thus says the Lord of hosts; I am very jealous for Jerusalem and for Zion. [15] And I am extremely angry with the nations that are at ease; for while I was only a little angry, they made the disaster worse. [16] Therefore, thus says the Lord, I have returned to Jerusalem with compassion; my house shall be built in it, says the Lord of hosts, and the measuring line shall be stretched out over Jerusalem. [17] Proclaim further: Thus says the Lord of hosts: My cities shall again overflow with prosperity; the Lord will again comfort Zion and again choose Jerusalem. (Zechariah 1:8-17)

The following passage is from the *Annals of Ashurbanipal*, it is also an interpreted dream:

In the midst of that night when I invoked her, then a seer slept, and dreamed a remarkable dream, and during the night Ishtar spoke to him, and he repeated it to me. Thus: "Ishtar dwelling in Arbela, entered, and right and lift she was surrounded with glory, holding a bow in her hand, projecting a powerful arrow on making war, her countenance was set. She like a mother bearing a child, was in pain with thee, she brought thee forth. Ishtar exalted of the gods, appointeth thee a decree. Thus: "Carry off to make spoil, the place before thee set, I will come to . . ." The Goddess of Goddesses she repeateth to thee thus: "Thee I will guard, then I will rest in the place of the temple of Nebo, eat food, drink wine, music appoint, glorify my divinity, until I go, and this message shall be accomplished.

Source: Cylinder B.5.49-67 from George Smith, *History of Assurbanipal* (Edinburgh: Williams and Norgate, 1881), 123–125.

Questions for Group Discussion

1. What are the purposes of biblical prophecy?
2. Why were some ancient Israelites invested in the notion of God's judgment?
3. What do we learn of the character of the biblical prophets?

Questions for Reflection

1. The biblical prophets are advocates for the poor and oppressed. How does this help us better understand the role of divine judgment in the Bible?

2. Do the Hebrew prophets have more to say about their present political situations or the end of the world?

8

An Alternative Worldview: Israel's Wisdom Literature and Esther

Summary and Learning Objectives

1. While the authors of biblical wisdom literature believe that God is deeply involved in the way the world is structured, they struggle to explain this structure. The biblical books of wisdom are reflections and critiques of the created order and humanity's place within it. These reflections and critiques can offer a dark view of the human experience. They can also include simple and basic instructions for general well-being.

2. After reading this chapter (alongside chapter 8 of Sumney's text), the reader should be able *to identify questions related to theodicy.*

3. After reading this chapter (alongside chapter 8 of Sumney's text), the reader should be able *to speak to the purpose and limits of ancient proverbs.*

4. After reading this chapter (alongside chapter 8 of Sumney's text), the reader should be able *to indentify a few elements of determinism in Ecclesiastes.*

5. After reading this chapter (alongside chapter 8 of Sumney's text), the reader should be able *to describe a few aspects of Jewish life in Persia.*

Key Terms

Determinism   The belief that all events are caused by things that happened before them and that people have no substantial ability to make choices to change fate.

Job   Leading character in the book of Job. God allows terrible things to happen to him and his family as a demonstration that Job's faithfulness to God is not only because God blesses him. This book raises the issue of theodicy.

Satan   A word that means adversary or opposer. In the book of Job this figure in the heavenly court serves as the prosecuting attorney in heaven.

Theodicy   The problem of the presence of evil and basic unfairness that exist in a world made by an all-good God. It is sometimes expressed by a person asking why bad things happen to good people.

Key Themes

▶ Ancient biblical conceptions of the afterlife were dissimilar to our modern mythologies

▶ Wisdom literature creates space to question God's purpose and his ordering of creation

▶ Many proverbs have a rather limited view on the value of women

Primary Text

The Satan

Before the word "satan" became a name, it simply meant "adversary" (keep in mind that Satan is never mentioned in Genesis 3). Psalm 38:20 uses this word (in the plural) in the following verse: "Those who render me evil for good are my **adversaries** because I follow after good." You see here that the word does not indicate a specific personality. Rather, "satans" are those that oppose God's people. This speaks well of the function of "the satan" in Job. In Job 1:6-12, we get the picture of a heavenly assembly of divine beings. In this "court" the accuser (the "satan") functions as an adversary of Job before God who is acting as the divine judge.

> ⁶ One day the heavenly beings came to present themselves before the Lord, and Satan

also came among them. ⁷ The Lord said to Satan, "Where have you come from?" Satan answered the Lord, "From going to and fro on the earth, and from walking up and down on it." ⁸ The Lord said to Satan, "Have you considered my servant Job? There is no one like him on the earth, a blameless and upright man who fears God and turns away from evil." ⁹ Then Satan answered the Lord, "Does Job fear God for nothing? ¹⁰ Have you not put a fence around him and his house and all that he has, on every side? You have blessed the work of his hands, and his possessions have increased in the land. ¹¹ But stretch out your hand now, and touch all that he has, and he will curse you to your face." ¹² The Lord said to Satan, "Very well, all that he has is in your power; only do not stretch out your hand against him!" So Satan went out from the presence of the Lord. (Job 1:6-12)

We see a similar setting described in Psalm 82. In this case, it is the Lord who is pronouncing judgment on the other deities in the room.

> ¹ God has taken his place in the divine council;
>   in the midst of the gods he holds
>   judgment:
> ² "How long will you judge unjustly
>   and show partiality to the wicked?
> ³ Give justice to the weak and the orphan;
>   maintain the right of the lowly and the
>   destitute.
> ⁴ Rescue the weak and the needy;
>   deliver them from the hand of the wicked."
> ⁵ They have neither knowledge nor
>   understanding,
>   they walk around in darkness;

all the foundations of the earth are shaken.
⁶ I say, "You are gods,
    children of the Most High, all of you;
⁷ nevertheless, you shall die like mortals,
    and fall like any prince."
⁸ Rise up, O God, judge the earth;
    for all the nations belong to you!
(Psalm 82)

What are the similarities between these two texts? How does God act differently between these two scenes?

A Despondent Man Talks to God

Job is the victim of a violent loss of life and well-being. He loses his good standing, family, wealth, and health. This leads him to question God about why such a horrible fate befell him when he had been faithful to a good and powerful God. If he had been righteous, and if the Lord is good and powerful, why shouldn't he expect God's favor? This is a question that we call "theodicy." He cries out about his suffering in this excerpt from Job 30:16-31:

¹⁶ "And now my soul is poured out within me; days of affliction have taken hold of me. ¹⁷ The night racks my bones, and the pain that gnaws me takes no rest. ¹⁸ With violence he seizes my garment; he grasps me by the collar of my tunic. ¹⁹ He has cast me into the mire, and I have become like dust and ashes. ²⁰ I cry to you and you do not answer me; I stand, and you merely look at me. ²¹ You have turned cruel to me; with the might of your hand you persecute me. ²² You lift me up on the wind, you make me ride on it, and you toss me about in the roar of the storm. ²³ I know that you will bring me to death, and to the house

appointed for all living. ²⁴ "Surely one does not turn against the needy, when in disaster they cry for help. ²⁵ Did I not weep for those whose day was hard? Was not my soul grieved for the poor? ²⁶ But when I looked for good, evil came; and when I waited for light, darkness came. ²⁷ My inward parts are in turmoil, and are never still; days of affliction come to meet me. ²⁸ I go about in sunless gloom; I stand up in the assembly and cry for help. ²⁹ I am a brother of jackals, and a companion of ostriches. ³⁰ My skin turns black and falls from me, and my bones burn with heat. ³¹ My lyre is turned to mourning, and my pipe to the voice of those who weep."

You can read of God's answer to Job in Job 38:1—40:5 and 40:6—42:6. A parallel to this poetic story is found in an Akkadian text (AO 4462) from the third millennium B.C.E. In this fragmentary text, a suffering man complains to his god. This god replies, "Your disease is under control, let your heart not be despondent . . . You must never, till the end of time, forget your god, your creator, now that you are favored." The man replies, "May your servant's supplication reach your heart." (Source: W. G. Lambert, "A Further Attempt at the Babylonian 'Man and His God,'" in *Language, Literature, and History: Philological and Historical Studies Presented to Erica Reiner*, AOS 67 [New Haven: American Oriental Society, 1987], 187–202.)

The Ways of the Wise and Foolish

The book of Proverbs likens life to two paths. A wise person will choose the path of hard work, honesty, and fear of the Lord; the fool will choose the against these virtues. Consider Proverbs chapter 2:

[1] My child, if you accept my words
  and treasure up my commandments
    within you,
[2] making your ear attentive to wisdom
  and inclining your heart to understanding;
[3] if you indeed cry out for insight,
  and raise your voice for understanding;
[4] if you seek it like silver,
  and search for it as for hidden treasures—
[5] then you will understand the fear of the Lord
  and find the knowledge of God.
[6] For the Lord gives wisdom;
  from his mouth come knowledge and
    understanding;
[7] he stores up sound wisdom for the upright;
  he is a shield to those who walk
    blamelessly,
[8] guarding the paths of justice
  and preserving the way of his faithful ones.
[9] Then you will understand righteousness and
    justice
  and equity, every good path;
[10] for wisdom will come into your heart,
  and knowledge will be pleasant to your soul;
[11] prudence will watch over you;
  and understanding will guard you.
[12] It will save you from the way of evil,
  from those who speak perversely,
[13] who forsake the paths of uprightness
  to walk in the ways of darkness,
[14] who rejoice in doing evil
  and delight in the perverseness of evil;
[15] those whose paths are crooked,
  and who are devious in their ways.
[16] You will be saved from the loose woman,
  from the adulteress with her smooth
    words,
[17] who forsakes the partner of her youth

and forgets her sacred covenant;
[18] for her way leads down to death,
  and her paths to the shades;
[19] those who go to her never come back,
  nor do they regain the paths of life.
[20] Therefore walk in the way of the good,
  and keep to the paths of the just.
[21] For the upright will abide in the land,
  and the innocent will remain in it;
[22] but the wicked will be cut off from the land,
  and the treacherous will be rooted out of it.

Now compare the similarities of style and content to these Summarian proverbs: Like those in the Bible, these are also context dependent, so that they can contain seemingly contradictory statements at times.

Who can compete with righteousness? It creates life (1.1).

A heart never created hatred; speech created hatred (1.72-73).

A disorderly son —his mother should not have given birth to him. His god should not have created him (1.157).

Marrying is human. Having children is divine (1.160).

A malicious wife living in the house is worse than all diseases (Collection 1.154).

When I married a malicious husband, when I bore a malicious son, an unhappy heart was assigned to me (1.51).

In my heart you are a human being, but in my eyes you are not a man (1.95).

A heart never created hatred; speech created hatred (1.105).

To be sick is acceptable; to be pregnant is painful; but to be pregnant and sick is just too much (1.193-94).

Tell a lie and then tell the truth: it will be considered a lie (2.128).

Source: J. A. Black, G. Cunningham, E. Fluckiger-Hawker, E. Robson, and G. Zólyomi, *The Electronic Text Corpus of Sumerian Literature;* http://www-etcsl.orient.ox.ac.uk/

Death and the Afterlife in Ecclesiastes

Consider the following passage from Ecclesiastes 9:1-12. Read it with special attention to verses 9:5-6 and verse 10:

> [1] All this I laid to heart, examining it all, how the righteous and the wise and their deeds are in the hand of God; whether it is love or hate one does not know. Everything that confronts them [2] is vanity, since the same fate comes to all, to the righteous and the wicked, to the good and the evil, to the clean and the unclean, to those who sacrifice and those who do not sacrifice. As are the good, so are the sinners; those who swear are like those who shun an oath. [3] This is an evil in all that happens under the sun, that the same fate comes to everyone. Moreover, the hearts of all are full of evil; madness is in their hearts while they live, and after that they go to the dead.
> [4] But whoever is joined with all the living has hope, for a living dog is better than a dead lion. [5] The living know that they will die, but the dead know nothing; they have no more reward, and even the memory of them is lost. [6] Their love and their hate and their envy have already perished; never again will they have any share in all that happens under the sun. [7] Go, eat your bread with enjoyment, and drink your wine with a merry heart; for God has long ago approved what you do. [8] Let your garments always be white; do not let oil be lacking on your head. [9] Enjoy life with the wife whom you love, all the days of your vain life that are given you under the sun, because that is your portion in life and in your toil at which you toil under the sun. [10] Whatever your hand finds to do, do with your might; for there is no work or thought or knowledge or wisdom in Sheol, to which you are going.
> [11] Again I saw that under the sun the race is not to the swift, nor the battle to the strong, nor bread to the wise, nor riches to the intelligent, nor favor to the skillful; but time and chance happen to them all. [12] For no one can anticipate the time of disaster. Like fish taken in a cruel net, and like birds caught in a snare, so mortals are snared at a time of calamity, when it suddenly falls upon them.

The preacher of this sermon puts forth a view of the afterlife without the common notion of eternal torment or bliss that we might expect to find. This view leads the preacher to exhort a full life here and now. Indeed he says, "So I commend enjoyment, for there is nothing better for people under the sun than to eat, and drink, and enjoy themselves, for this will go with them in their toil through the days of life that God gives them under the sun" (8:15). How does this view compare with view offered in 1 Samuel 28:1-18?

> [1] In those days the Philistines gathered their forces for war, to fight against Israel. Achish said to David, "You know, of course, that you and your men are to go

out with me in the army." [2] David said to Achish, "Very well, then you shall know what your servant can do." Achish said to David, "Very well, I will make you my bodyguard for life." [3] Now Samuel had died, and all Israel had mourned for him and buried him in Ramah, his own city. Saul had expelled the mediums and the wizards from the land. [4] The Philistines assembled, and came and encamped at Shunem. Saul gathered all Israel, and they encamped at Gilboa. [5] When Saul saw the army of the Philistines, he was afraid, and his heart trembled greatly. [6] When Saul inquired of the Lord, the Lord did not answer him, not by dreams, or by Urim, or by prophets.

[7] Then Saul said to his servants, "Seek out for me a woman who is a medium, so that I may go to her and inquire of her." His servants said to him, "There is a medium at Endor." [8] So Saul disguised himself and put on other clothes and went there, he and two men with him. They came to the woman by night. And he said, "Consult a spirit for me, and bring up for me the one whom I name to you." [9] The woman said to him, "Surely you know what Saul has done, how he has cut off the mediums and the wizards from the land. Why then are you laying a snare for my life to bring about my death?" [10] But Saul swore to her by the Lord, "As the Lord lives, no punishment shall come upon you for this thing." [11] Then the woman said, "Whom shall I bring up for you?" He answered, "Bring up Samuel for me." [12] When the woman saw Samuel, she cried out with a loud voice; and the woman said to Saul, "Why have you deceived me? You

are Saul!" [13] The king said to her, "Have no fear; what do you see?" The woman said to Saul, "I see a divine being coming up out of the ground." [14] He said to her, "What is his appearance?" She said, "An old man is coming up; he is wrapped in a robe." So Saul knew that it was Samuel, and he bowed with his face to the ground, and did obeisance.

[15] Then Samuel said to Saul, "Why have you disturbed me by bringing me up?" Saul answered, "I am in great distress, for the Philistines are warring against me, and God has turned away from me and answers me no more, either by prophets or by dreams; so I have summoned you to tell me what I should do." [16] Samuel said, "Why then do you ask me, since the Lord has turned from you and become your enemy? [17] The Lord has done to you just as he spoke by me; for the Lord has torn the kingdom out of your hand, and given it to your neighbor, David. [18] Because you did not obey the voice of the Lord, and did not carry out his fierce wrath against Amalek, therefore the Lord has done this thing to you today.

What does this story suggest about life after death? What does this view of the afterlife have in common with the view of Ecclesiastes? In what ways do these texts differ?

Ecclesiastes on Determinism

The preacher of Ecclesiastes believes that humans have no control over their fate. Perhaps God determines all (compare with Ecclesiastes 3:1-11), or perhaps it doesn't matter because all people as destined for the same fate. This is a form of determinism. Consider Ecclesiastes 6:1-9:

[1] There is an evil that I have seen under the sun, and it lies heavy upon humankind: [2] those to whom God gives wealth, possessions, and honor, so that they lack nothing of all that they desire, yet God does not enable them to enjoy these things, but a stranger enjoys them. This is vanity; it is a grievous ill. [3] A man may beget a hundred children, and live many years; but however many are the days of his years, if he does not enjoy life's good things, or has no burial, I say that a stillborn child is better off than he. [4] For it comes into vanity and goes into darkness, and in darkness its name is covered; [5] moreover it has not seen the sun or known anything; yet it finds rest rather than he. [6] Even though he should live a thousand years twice over, yet enjoy no good—do not all go to one place?

[7] All human toil is for the mouth, yet the appetite is not satisfied. [8] For what advantage have the wise over fools? And what do the poor have who know how to conduct themselves before the living? [9] Better is the sight of the eyes than the wandering of desire; this also is vanity and a chasing after wind.

Compare Ecclesiastes determinism to these fatalistic and pessimistic Sumerian proverbs:

Fate is a dog—well able to bite. Like dirty rags, it clings, saying: "Who is my man? Let him know it" (2.11).

Fate is a raging storm blowing over the Land (2.13).

Fate is a dog walking always behind a man (2.14).

Source: J. A. Black, G. Cunningham, E. Fluckiger-Hawker, E. Robson, and G. Zólyomi, *The Electronic Text Corpus of Sumerian Literature;* http://www-etcsl.orient.ox.ac.uk/

Jewish Culture in Persia

While the story of Esther is not a factual report of historical people, it might offer valuable insights about life in the ancient world. Read chapters three and four of Esther and look for cultural assumptions and practices:

[1] After these things King Ahasuerus promoted Haman son of Hammedatha the Agagite, and advanced him and set his seat above all the officials who were with him. [2] And all the king's servants who were at the king's gate bowed down and did obeisance to Haman; for the king had so commanded concerning him. But Mordecai did not bow down or do obeisance. [3] Then the king's servants who were at the king's gate said to Mordecai, "Why do you disobey the king's command?" [4] When they spoke to him day after day and he would not listen to them, they told Haman, in order to see whether Mordecai's words would avail; for he had told them that he was a Jew. [5] When Haman saw that Mordecai did not bow down or do obeisance to him, Haman was infuriated. [6] But he thought it beneath him to lay hands on Mordecai alone. So, having been told who Mordecai's people were, Haman plotted to destroy all the Jews, the people of Mordecai, throughout the whole kingdom of Ahasuerus.

[7] In the first month, which is the month of Nisan, in the twelfth year of King

Ahasuerus, they cast Pur—which means "the lot"—before Haman for the day and for the month, and the lot fell on the thirteenth day of the twelfth month, which is the month of Adar. [8] Then Haman said to King Ahasuerus, "There is a certain people scattered and separated among the peoples in all the provinces of your kingdom; their laws are different from those of every other people, and they do not keep the king's laws, so that it is not appropriate for the king to tolerate them. [9] If it pleases the king, let a decree be issued for their destruction, and I will pay ten thousand talents of silver into the hands of those who have charge of the king's business, so that they may put it into the king's treasuries." [10] So the king took his signet ring from his hand and gave it to Haman son of Hammedatha the Agagite, the enemy of the Jews. [11] The king said to Haman, "The money is given to you, and the people as well, to do with them as it seems good to you." [12] Then the king's secretaries were summoned on the thirteenth day of the first month, and an edict, according to all that Haman commanded, was written to the king's satraps and to the governors over all the provinces and to the officials of all the peoples, to every province in its own script and every people in its own language; it was written in the name of King Ahasuerus and sealed with the king's ring. [13] Letters were sent by couriers to all the king's provinces, giving orders to destroy, to kill, and to annihilate all Jews, young and old, women and children, in one day, the thirteenth day of the twelfth month, which is the month of Adar,

and to plunder their goods. [14] A copy of the document was to be issued as a decree in every province by proclamation, calling on all the peoples to be ready for that day. [15] The couriers went quickly by order of the king, and the decree was issued in the citadel of Susa. The king and Haman sat down to drink; but the city of Susa was thrown into confusion.

4 [1] When Mordecai learned all that had been done, Mordecai tore his clothes and put on sackcloth and ashes, and went through the city, wailing with a loud and bitter cry; [2] he went up to the entrance of the king's gate, for no one might enter the king's gate clothed with sackcloth. [3] In every province, wherever the king's command and his decree came, there was great mourning among the Jews, with fasting and weeping and lamenting, and most of them lay in sackcloth and ashes. [4] When Esther's maids and her eunuchs came and told her, the queen was deeply distressed; she sent garments to clothe Mordecai, so that he might take off his sackcloth; but he would not accept them.

[5] Then Esther called for Hathach, one of the king's eunuchs, who had been appointed to attend her, and ordered him to go to Mordecai to learn what was happening and why. [6] Hathach went out to Mordecai in the open square of the city in front of the king's gate, [7] and Mordecai told him all that had happened to him, and the exact sum of money that Haman had promised to pay into the king's treasuries for the destruction of the Jews. [8] Mordecai also gave him a copy of the written decree

issued in Susa for their destruction, that he might show it to Esther, explain it to her, and charge her to go to the king to make supplication to him and entreat him for her people. [9] Hathach went and told Esther what Mordecai had said. [10] Then Esther spoke to Hathach and gave him a message for Mordecai, saying, [11] "All the king's servants and the people of the king's provinces know that if any man or woman goes to the king inside the inner court without being called, there is but one law—all alike are to be put to death. Only if the king holds out the golden scepter to someone, may that person live. I myself have not been called to come in to the king for thirty days." [12] When they told Mordecai what Esther had said, [13] Mordecai told them to reply to Esther, "Do not think that in the king's palace you will escape any more than all the other Jews. [14] For if you keep silence at such a time as this, relief and deliverance will rise for the Jews from another quarter, but you and your father's family will perish. Who knows? Perhaps you have come to royal dignity for just such a time as this." [15] Then Esther said in reply to Mordecai, [16] "Go, gather all the Jews to be found in Susa, and hold a fast on my behalf, and neither eat nor drink for three days, night or day. I and my maids will also fast as you do. After that I will go to the king, though it is against the law; and if I perish, I perish." [17] Mordecai then went away and did everything as Esther had ordered him. (Esther 3:1—4:17)

What sort of government is in place in this story? Where in the Jews rank in this particular power system? What sort of power did women have over their own lives in this system? What some other cultural similarities and differences between this world and the modern world?

Questions for Group Discussion

1. How can the pursuit of wisdom change one's fate according to Proverbs?
2. How do the views of the proverbs discussed above differ from each other and from the view of Ecclesiastes?
3. How do ancient conceptions "the satan" differ from those in modern mythologies?

Questions for Reflection

1. Do you find any of the ancient texts discussed here disturbing? If so, why?

2. How might a person's view of the afterlife affect his or her actions in the present?

9

Israel's Response to God: The Psalms and the Song of Solomon

Summary and Learning Objectives

1. There is perhaps no better window into Israel's life of worship and beliefs than the biblical psalms. We are given an altogether unique view of this culture with the Song of Solomon. After reading this chapter (alongside chapter 9 of Sumney's text), the reader should be able *to identify at least five different literary types of psalms.*

2. After reading this chapter (alongside chapter 9 of Sumney's text), the reader should be able *to explain the various purposes of the different psalms discussed in this chapter.*

3. After reading this chapter (alongside chapter 9 of Sumney's text), the reader should be able *to identify a few different types of parallelism in Hebrew poetry.*

4. After reading this chapter (alongside chapter 9 of Sumney's text), the reader should be able *to interpret the metaphor "son" when used in a royal psalm.*

5. After reading this chapter (alongside chapter 9 of Sumney's text), the reader should be able *to interpret the metaphor "brother" when used in erotic poetry.*

Key Terms

Didactic psalms   Psalms designed to teach about God and how God wants people to live.

Imprecatory psalms   Psalms that ask God to harm others and put curses on one's enemies.

Parallelism   A literary technique used in Hebrew poetry that thematically and structurally links two or more lines.

Royal psalms   Psalms that deal with particular moments in a king's career, thanking God or asking God's blessing for the king's future.

Key Themes

▶ The psalms contain some of the most raw emotional content but within a formal structure

▶ Many psalms served a particularly formal function within the life of Israel

▶ Erotic poetry seems to have been popular in the ancient world, but is only represented once in the biblical canon

Primary Text

Psalm Literary Types

The following poems are complete psalms from the Bible. Each represents a different literary type. As you read, look for the similarities and differences in theme and tone. One thing shared by all of the following is the poetic use of parallelism. In short, this is a process of setting two or more concepts in juxtaposition so that they become mutually interpretative.

EXAMPLE OF A THANKSGIVING PSALM (PSALM 65)

[1] Praise is due to you,
     O God, in Zion;
and to you shall vows be performed,
     [2] O you who answer prayer!
To you all flesh shall come.
[3] When deeds of iniquity overwhelm us,
     you forgive our transgressions.
[4] Happy are those whom you choose and bring near
     to live in your courts.
We shall be satisfied with the goodness of your house,
     your holy temple.
[5] By awesome deeds you answer us with deliverance,

O God of our salvation;
you are the hope of all the ends of the earth
     and of the farthest seas.
[6] By your strength you established the mountains;
     you are girded with might.
[7] You silence the roaring of the seas,
     the roaring of their waves,
     the tumult of the peoples.
[8] Those who live at earth's farthest bounds are awed by your signs;
you make the gateways of the morning and the evening shout for joy.
[9] You visit the earth and water it,
     you greatly enrich it;
the river of God is full of water;
     you provide the people with grain,
     for so you have prepared it.
[10] You water its furrows abundantly,
     settling its ridges,
softening it with showers,
     and blessing its growth.
[11] You crown the year with your bounty;
     your wagon tracks overflow with richness.
[12] The pastures of the wilderness overflow,
     the hills gird themselves with joy,
[13] the meadows clothe themselves with flocks,
     the valleys deck themselves with grain,
     they shout and sing together for joy.

EXAMPLE OF A DIDACTIC PSALM (PSALM 32)

[1] Happy are those whose transgression is forgiven,
whose sin is covered.
[2] Happy are those to whom the Lord imputes no iniquity,
     and in whose spirit there is no deceit.
[3] While I kept silence, my body wasted away

through my groaning all day long.
⁴ For day and night your hand was heavy upon
me;
my strength was dried up as by the heat of
summer.   *Selah*
⁵ Then I acknowledged my sin to you,
and I did not hide my iniquity;
I said, "I will confess my transgressions to the
Lord,"
and you forgave the guilt of my sin.   *Selah*
⁶ Therefore let all who are faithful
offer prayer to you;
at a time of distress, the rush of mighty waters
shall not reach them.
⁷ You are a hiding place for me;
you preserve me from trouble;
you surround me with glad cries of
deliverance.   *Selah*
⁸ I will instruct you and teach you the way you
should go;
I will counsel you with my eye upon you.
⁹ Do not be like a horse or a mule, without
understanding,
whose temper must be curbed with bit and
bridle,
else it will not stay near you.
¹⁰ Many are the torments of the wicked,
but steadfast love surrounds those who
trust in the Lord.
¹¹ Be glad in the Lord and rejoice, O righteous,
and shout for joy, all you upright in heart.

EXAMPLE OF A ROYAL PSALM (PSALM 2)

¹ Why do the nations conspire,
and the peoples plot in vain?
² The kings of the earth set themselves,
and the rulers take counsel together,
against the Lord and his anointed, saying,

³ "Let us burst their bonds asunder,
and cast their cords from us."
⁴ He who sits in the heavens laughs;
the Lord has them in derision.
⁵ Then he will speak to them in his wrath,
and terrify them in his fury, saying,
⁶ "I have set my king on Zion, my holy hill."
⁷ I will tell of the decree of the Lord:
He said to me, "You are my son;
today I have begotten you.
⁸ Ask of me, and I will make the nations your
heritage,
and the ends of the earth your possession.
⁹ You shall break them with a rod of iron,
and dash them in pieces like a potter's
vessel."
¹⁰ Now therefore, O kings, be wise;
be warned, O rulers of the earth.
¹¹ Serve the Lord with fear,
with trembling ¹² kiss his feet,
or he will be angry, and you will perish in the
way;
for his wrath is quickly kindled.
Happy are all who take refuge in him.

EXAMPLE OF A LAMENT PSALM (PSALM 7)

¹ O Lord my God, in you I take refuge;
save me from all my pursuers, and deliver
me,
² or like a lion they will tear me apart;
they will drag me away, with no one to
rescue.
³ O Lord my God, if I have done this,
if there is wrong in my hands,
⁴ if I have repaid my ally with harm
or plundered my foe without cause,
⁵ then let the enemy pursue and overtake me,
trample my life to the ground,

and lay my soul in the dust. *Selah*

6 Rise up, O Lord, in your anger;

lift yourself up against the fury of my
enemies;

awake, O my God; you have appointed a
judgment.

7 Let the assembly of the peoples be gathered
around you,

and over it take your seat on high.

8 The Lord judges the peoples;

judge me, O Lord, according to my
righteousness

and according to the integrity that is in
me.

9 O let the evil of the wicked come to an end,

but establish the righteous,

you who test the minds and hearts,

O righteous God.

10 God is my shield,

who saves the upright in heart.

11 God is a righteous judge,

and a God who has indignation every day.

12 If one does not repent, God will whet his
sword;

he has bent and strung his bow;

13 he has prepared his deadly weapons,

making his arrows fiery shafts.

14 See how they conceive evil,

and are pregnant with mischief,

and bring forth lies.

15 They make a pit, digging it out,

and fall into the hole that they have made.

16 Their mischief returns upon their own heads,

and on their own heads their violence
descends.

17 I will give to the Lord the thanks due to his
righteousness,

and sing praise to the name of the Lord,
the Most High.

EXAMPLE OF A CURSING (IMPRECATORY) PSALM (PSALM 109)

1 Do not be silent, O God of my praise.

2 For wicked and deceitful mouths are opened
against me,

speaking against me with lying tongues.

3 They beset me with words of hate,

and attack me without cause.

4 In return for my love they accuse me,

even while I make prayer for them.

5 So they reward me evil for good,

and hatred for my love.

6 They say, "Appoint a wicked man against him;

let an accuser stand on his right.

7 When he is tried, let him be found guilty;

let his prayer be counted as sin.

8 May his days be few;

may another seize his position.

9 May his children be orphans,

and his wife a widow.

10 May his children wander about and beg;

may they be driven out of the ruins they
inhabit.

11 May the creditor seize all that he has;

may strangers plunder the fruits of his toil.

12 May there be no one to do him a kindness,

nor anyone to pity his orphaned children.

13 May his posterity be cut off;

may his name be blotted out in the second
generation.

14 May the iniquity of his father be remembered
before the Lord,

and do not let the sin of his mother be
blotted out.

¹⁵ Let them be before the Lord continually,
    and may his memory be cut off from the
      earth.
¹⁶ For he did not remember to show kindness,
    but pursued the poor and needy
    and the brokenhearted to their death.
¹⁷ He loved to curse; let curses come on him.
    He did not like blessing; may it be far from
      him.
¹⁸ He clothed himself with cursing as his coat,
    may it soak into his body like water,
    like oil into his bones.
¹⁹ May it be like a garment that he wraps
    around himself,
    like a belt that he wears every day."
²⁰ May that be the reward of my accusers from
    the Lord,
    of those who speak evil against my life.
²¹ But you, O Lord my Lord,
    act on my behalf for your name's sake;
    because your steadfast love is good, deliver
      me.
²² For I am poor and needy,
    and my heart is pierced within me.
²³ I am gone like a shadow at evening;
    I am shaken off like a locust.
²⁴ My knees are weak through fasting;
    my body has become gaunt.
²⁵ I am an object of scorn to my accusers;
    when they see me, they shake their heads.
²⁶ Help me, O Lord my God!
    Save me according to your steadfast love.
²⁷ Let them know that this is your hand;
    you, O Lord, have done it.
²⁸ Let them curse, but you will bless.
    Let my assailants be put to shame; may
      your servant be glad.
²⁹ May my accusers be clothed with dishonor;

may they be wrapped in their own shame
    as in a mantle.
³⁰ With my mouth I will give great thanks to
    the Lord;
    I will praise him in the midst of the
      throng.
³¹ For he stands at the right hand of the needy,
    to save them from those who would con
      demn them to death.

Non-Biblical Psalms

The following is a Psalm of Praise to Ishtar. This looks like a hymn of praise that then turns to lament at line 42. Below is the first eight lines of praise and then some lines of the lamentation.

> I pray unto you, lady of ladies, goddess of
>   goddesses!
> O Ishtar, queen of all peoples, directress of all
>   people!
> O Irini, you are raised on high, mistress of the
>   Spirits
> You are mighty, you have sovereign power,
>   exalted is your name!
> You are the light of heaven and earth, O valiant
>   daughter of the Moon-god.
> Ruler of weapons, arbitress of the battle!
> Framer of all decrees, wearer of the crown of
>   domination!
> O lady majestic is your rank, over all the gods
>   exalted!
>
> . . .
>
> Where you look with pity, the dead man lives
>   again, the sick is healed;
> The afflicted is saved from his affliction, when
>   he beholds his face!
> I, your servant, sorrowful, sighing, and in dis-
>   tress cry unto you.

Look upon me, O my lady, and accept my
    supplication,
Truly pity me, and listen to my prayer! Cry
    unto me "It is enough!" and let your spirit
    be appeased

. . .

How long, O lady, shall my enemies persecute
    me?
How long shall they devise evil in rebellion and
    wickedness,
And in my pursuits and my pleasures shall they
    rage against me?
How long, O lady, shall the ravenous demon
    pursue me?
They have caused me continuous affliction, but
    I have praised you.
The weak have become strong, but I am weak;
I am sated like a flood which the evil wind
    makes to rage.
My heart has taken wing and has flown away
    like a bird of the heavens;
I moan like a dove, night and day.
I am made desolate, and I weep bitterly;
With grief and woe my spirit is distressed.
What have I done. O my god and my goddess?

. . .

Let my prayer and my supplication come unto
    you,
And let your great mercy be upon me,
That those who behold me in the street may
    magnify your name before all people!
Ishtar is exalted! Ishtar is queen!
My lady is exalted! My lady is queen!

Source: L. W. King, *The Seven Tablets of
Creation*, Luzac's Semitic Text and Translation Series, vol. 12 (London: Luzac and Co.,
1902), 222–34, lines 1–8, 40–45, 56–67 99–104;

http://www.etana.org/sites/default/files/core-
texts/14907.pdf

This is an enthronement Psalm from Enuma
Elish 6.99-111. In the enthronement Psalms, the
king is sometimes called the son of God. Compare
this with Psalm 2, included above:

Most exalted be the Son, our avenger;
Let his sovereignty be surpassing, having no
    rival.
May he shepherd the black-headed ones
    [humans], his creatures.
To the end of days, without forgetting, let them
    acclaim his ways.
May he establish for his fathers the great
    food-offerings;
Their support they shall furnish, shall tend
    their sanctuaries.

Source: Speiser, *Ancient Near Eastern Texts
Relating to the Old Testament*, 2nd ed., ANET
69, ed. James B. Pritchard (Princeton: Princeton University Press, 1955).

The Dead Sea Scrolls included a handful of
extra psalms that are not found in the final form of
the biblical canon. Consider this "psalm of David":

Hallelujah! A psalm of David, son of Jesse.
I was smaller than my brothers,
    youngest of my father's sons.
So he made me a shepherd for his sheep,
    a ruler over his goats.
My hands fashioned a pipe, my fingers a lyre,
    and I glorified the Lord.
I said to myself, "The mountains do not testify
    to Him,
    nor do the hills proclaim."
So-echo my words, O trees,
    O sheep, my deeds!

Ah, but who can proclaim,
> who declare the deeds of the Lord?

God has seen all,
> heard and attended to everything.

He sent his prophet to anoint me,
> even Samuel, to raise me up.

My brothers went forth to meet him:
> handsome of figure, wondrous of
> > appearance,

tall were they of stature, so beautiful their
> hair—
> > yet the Lord God did not choose them.

No, He sent and took me who followed the
> flock,
> > and anointed me with the holy oil.

He set me as prince to His people,
> vacat ruler over the children of His
> > covenant.

Source: 11Q5 Col. XXVIII (Psalm 151) from
M. Wise, M Abegg, and E. Cook, eds., *The
Dead Sea Scrolls: A New Translation* (San Fran-
cisco: HarperSanFrancisco, 1996), 448.

Erotic Poetry

The erotic poetry of Song of Solomon (also called
Song of Songs) is unique in the Bible. But such erotic
poetry was not unique in the ancient world. Here is
an erotic poem from Egypt (unfortunately, this text
is fragmentary):

1. my love. The desire rises within me that
I may behold the food . . . . the salt, the
strong liquors. . . .

2. that which is sweet in the mouth is
like the gall of a bird. I smell, I snuff up.
Solitary is he who . . . . my heart, I find him
whom Amen hath given to me for

3. ever and ever. *Section.* Thou fair
one ! my heart . . . . when thou wast in thy
chamber. Thy arm was laid upon my arm;
thou didst survey

4. thy love. I (poured forth) my heart
to thee, in the . . . . my . . . . in the night. I
was as one in my

5. bower. Yea! art not thou the strength
of (my) life, the joy thou didst strengthen
my heart, to seek

6. thee. *Section.* The voice of the swal-
low resounds. It saith the earth is enlightened. How do I wait for thee, thou bird,
whilst thou chirpest (?)

7. I found my brother in his bed-cham-
ber. My heart . . . . go not far from me. Let
thy hand be in my hand. When I go to walk

8. let me be with thee, in every pleasant
place. Give me the choicest of fair things,
they . . . . not my heart.

Source: "Papyrus Harris 500" in C. W. Good-
win, *Transactions of the Society of Biblical
Archaeology, vols. 3–4,* (London: Society of Biblical Archaeology, 1874) 384–85.

What does the title "brother" mean in this context?
What does the metaphor "my heart" mean in this
context?

Questions for Group Discussion

1. What was the function (if any) of lament psalms within the life of Israel's worship?
2. What was the function (if any) of erotic poetry within the life of Israel's worship?
3. Why do you think that the Dead Sea Scrolls psalms did not make it into the biblical canon?

Questions for Reflection

1. What socio-economic class do you think that the Song of Solomon represents?

2. What was gained politically by calling the king the "son" of the deity?

10

Between the Testaments: From Alexander the Great to the Time of Jesus

Summary and Learning Objectives

1. The world into which Jesus was born was a complex of power systems and social dynamics. Before we can begin to understand Jesus' political context, we must learn about the intersections between Greek culture, Jewish leadership, and Roman politics. After reading this chapter (alongside chapter 10 of Sumney's text), the reader should be able *to identify a few ways that ancient biographers and historians bias their stories.*

2. After reading this chapter (alongside chapter 10 of Sumney's text), the reader should be able *to explain how and why the Pharisees fell from political influence in the Hasmonean state.*

3. After reading this chapter (alongside chapter 10 of Sumney's text), the reader should be able *to identify several features of Augustus's political program.*

Key Terms

Alexander the Great   Macedonian king who conquers southern Greece and then all the territory east to the border of India, reaching as far north as the Black Sea and as far south as North Africa. This created the largest empire the world had seen. In all these territories he instituted the policy of hellenization to form a common culture based on Greek culture.

Josephus   First-century Jewish writer who was a general in the revolt of 66–70 C.E. After his capture he becomes the historian for the Roman general Vespasian, who would soon be emperor. His writings give us important information about first-century Judaism and the war in which the Jerusalem temple was destroyed.

Judea   Name of the region around Jerusalem in the Greco-Roman period. In earlier times the same region was known as Judah.

Oral Torah   The oral tradition of the Pharisees that recorded the various interpretations of the law from the sages of their tradition. In about 200 C.E., these oral traditions were compiled in written form in the Mishnah.

Pharisees   One of the leading sects of Judaism in the first century C.E. They were known as expert interpreters of the law.

Sadducees   One of the leading sects of Judaism in the first century C.E. This group had many priests as members.

Key Themes

▶ Writing ancient history and biography is always an interpretive process
▶ Maintaining political power is often more difficult than acquiring it
▶ Negotiating power systems within a nation is often just as difficult as negotiating with foreign powers

Primary Text

Plutarch on Biography and Alexander the Great

The following excerpts come from Plutarch (c. 46–120 C.E.), a Greek historian and biographer. In the first paragraph, Plutarch explains how his writing differs from "history." The following excerpts tell of Alexander's early conquests in battle and the squabbles and insults that took place in Greek society. Notice how Plutarch's presentation of Alexander is focused in this short excerpt:

It being my purpose to write the lives of Alexander the king, and of Caesar, by whom Pompey was destroyed, the multitude of their great actions affords so large a field that I will make no other preface than to ask my readers not to complain if I do not thoroughly relate all their deeds or deal exhaustively with any one of them, but rather deal with most in summary fashion. It must be kept in mind that my design is not to write histories, but lives. And the most glorious deeds do not always furnish us with the clearest instances of virtue or vice in men; sometimes a matter of less importance, an expression or a jest, informs us better of their characters and inclinations, than the most famous sieges, the greatest armaments, or the bloodiest battles whatsoever. Therefore as portrait-painters are more exact in the lines and features of the face, in which the character is seen, than in the other parts of the body, so I must be allowed to give my more particular attention to the marks and indications of the souls of men, and while I endeavour by these to portray their lives, I may be free to leave more weighty matters and great battles to be treated of by others.

. . .

When Philip went on his expedition against Byzantium, he left Alexander, then sixteen years old, his regent in Macedonia, committing the charge of his seal to him. Alexander, so as not to sit idle, reduced the rebellious Maedi, and having taken their chief town by storm, drove out the barbarous inhabitants, and planting a colony of several nations in their room, called the place after his own name, Alexandropolis.

At the battle of Chaeronea, which his father fought against the Greeks, he is said to have been the first man that charged the Thebans' sacred band. And even in my remembrance, there stood an old oak near the river Cephisus, which people called Alexander's oak, because his tent was pitched under it. And not far off are to be seen the graves of the Macedonians who fell in that battle. This early bravery made Philip so fond of him, that nothing pleased him more than to hear his subjects call himself their general and Alexander their king. But the disorders of his family, chiefly caused by his new marriages and affairs (the troubles that began in the women's chambers spreading, so to say, to the whole kingdom), raised various complaints and differences between them, which the violence of Olympias, a woman of a jealous and implacable temper, made wider, by exasperating Alexander against his father. Among the rest, this accident contributed most to their falling out. At the wedding of Cleopatra, whom Philip fell in love with and married, she being much too young for him, her uncle Attalus in his drink asked the Macedonians to implore the gods to give them a lawful successor to the kingdom by his niece. This so irritated Alexander, that throwing one of the cups at his head, "You villain," said he, "what, am I then a bastard?" Then Philip, taking Attalus's part, rose up and would have run his son through; but by good fortune for them both, either his over-hasty rage, or the wine he had drunk, made his foot slip, so that he fell down on the floor. At which Alexander reproachfully insulted over him:

"See there," said he, "the man who makes preparations to pass out of Europe into Asia, overturned in passing from one seat to another." After this debauch, he and his mother Olympias withdrew from Philip's company, and when he had placed her in Epirus, he himself retired into Illyria. About this time, Demaratus the Corinthian, an old friend of the family, who had the freedom to say anything among them without offence, coming to visit Philip, after the first compliments and embraces were over, Philip asked him whether the Greeks were at amity with one another. "It ill becomes you," replied Demaratus, "to be so concerned about Greece, when you have involved your own house in so many dissensions and calamities." Philip was so convinced by this timely reproach, that he immediately sent for his son, and by Demaratus's mediation prevailed with him to return.

. . .

Alexander was but twenty years old when his father was murdered, and succeeded to a kingdom, beset on all sides with great dangers and rancorous enemies. For not only the barbarous nations that bordered on Macedonia were impatient of being governed by any but their own native princes, but Philip likewise, though he had been victorious over the Grecians, yet, as the time had not been sufficient for him to complete his conquest and accustom them to his sway, had simply left all things in a general disorder and confusion. It seemed to the Macedonians a very critical time; and some would have persuaded Alexander to give up all thought of retaining the Grecians in subjection by force of arms, and rather to apply himself to win back by gentle means the allegiance of the tribes who were designing revolt, and try the effect of indulgence in arresting the first motions towards revolution. But he rejected this counsel as weak and timorous, and looked upon it to be more prudence to secure himself by resolution and magnanimity, than, by seeming to truckle to any, to encourage all to trample on him. In pursuit of this opinion, he reduced the barbarians to tranquillity, and put an end to all fear of war from them, he gave rapid expedition into their country as far as the river Danube, where he gave Syrmus, King of the Triballians, an entire overthrow. And hearing the Thebans were in revolt, and the Athenians in correspondence with them, he immediately marched through the pass of Thermopylae, saying that to Demosthenes, who had called him a child while he was in Illyria and in the country of the Triballians, and a youth when he was in Thessaly, he would appear a man before the walls of Athens.

Source: John Dryden, trans., "Alexander" in *Plutarch's Lives*; http://classics.mit.edu/Plutarch/alexandr.html

What do we learn of Alexander's personality in these accounts? What do we learn about the political climate of Macedonia during his rise to power?

The Pharisee's Fall from Power

During the time of the Maccabees (or Hasmonean state), Israel was ruled by Jewish kings for the first time in centuries. Many of these kings functioned

as the high priest as well. Many in Israel saw this as an impurity. They believed the offices of kings and priest should be kept separate. The following excerpt from Josephus (a first-century Jewish historian) tells of how this controversy was debated during the rule of the Hyrcanus (about 100 years before Jesus was born). It also tells of how the Pharisees fell from political influence to the great benefit of the Sadducees.

4. Now it happened at this time, that not only those Jews who were at Jerusalem and in Judea were in prosperity, but also those of them that were at Alexandria, and in Egypt and Cyprus; for Cleopatra the queen was at variance with her son Ptolemy, who was called Lathyrus, and appointed for her generals Chelcias and Ananias, the sons of that Onias who built the temple in the prefecture of Heliopolis, like to that at Jerusalem, as we have elsewhere related. Cleopatra intrusted these men with her army, and did nothing without their advice, as Strabo of Cappadocia attests, when he saith thus, "Now the greater part, both those that came to Cyprus with us, and those that were sent afterward thither, revolted to Ptolemy immediately; only those that were called Onias's party, being Jews, continued faithful, because their countrymen Chelcias and Ananias were in chief favor with the queen." These are the words of Strabo.

5. However, this prosperous state of affairs moved the Jews to envy Hyrcanus; but they that were the worst disposed to him were the Pharisees, who were one of the sects of the Jews, as we have informed you already. These have so great a power over the multitude, that when they say

any thing against the king, or against the high priest, they are presently believed. Now Hyrcanus was a disciple of theirs, and greatly beloved by them. And when he once invited them to a feast, and entertained them very kindly, when he saw them in a good humor, he began to say to them, that they knew he was desirous to be a righteous man, and to do all things whereby he might please God, which was the profession of the Pharisees also. However, he desired, that if they observed him offending in any point, and going out of the right way, they would call him back and correct him. On which occasion they attested to his being entirely virtuous; with which commendation he was well pleased. But still there was one of his guests there, whose name was Eleazar, a man of an ill temper, and delighting in seditious practices. This man said, "Since thou desirest to know the truth, if thou wilt be righteous in earnest, lay down the high priesthood, and content thyself with the civil government of the people," And when he desired to know for what cause he ought to lay down the high priesthood, the other replied, "We have heard it from old men, that thy mother had been a captive under the reign of Antiochus Epiphanes." This story was false, and Hyrcanus was provoked against him; and all the Pharisees had a very great indignation against him.

6. Now there was one Jonathan, a very great friend of Hyrcanus's, but of the sect of the Sadducees, whose notions are quite contrary to those of the Pharisees. He told Hyrcanus that Eleazar had cast such a reproach upon him, according to the common

sentiments of all the Pharisees, and that this would be made manifest if he would but ask them the question, What punishment they thought this man deserved? for that he might depend upon it, that the reproach was not laid on him with their approbation, if they were for punishing him as his crime deserved. So the Pharisees made answer, that he deserved stripes and bonds, but that it did not seem right to punish reproaches with death. And indeed the Pharisees, even upon other occasions, are not apt to be severe in punishments. At this gentle sentence, Hyrcanus was very angry, and thought that this man reproached him by their approbation. It was this Jonathan who chiefly irritated him, and influenced him so far, that he made him leave the party of the Pharisees, and abolish the decrees they had imposed on the people, and to punish those that observed them. From this source arose that hatred which he and his sons met with from the multitude: but of these matters we shall speak hereafter. What I would now explain is this, that the Pharisees have delivered to the people a great many observances by succession from their fathers, which are not written in the laws of Moses; and for that reason it is that the Sadducees reject them, and say that we are to esteem those observances to be obligatory which are in the written word, but are not to observe what are derived from the tradition of our forefathers. And concerning these things it is that great disputes and differences have arisen among them, while the Sadducees are able to persuade none but the rich, and have not the populace obsequious to them, but the Pharisees have the multitude on their side. But about these two sects, and that of the Essens, I have treated accurately in the second book of Jewish affairs.

Source: Josephus, *Antiquities*, 13.4-6, trans. William Whiston; http://www.gutenberg.org/files/2848/2848-h/2848-h.htm

Josephus generally favors social elites in his histories and disfavors commoners. Given that the Pharisees were most supported by commoners, we might take Josephus's account with a bit of suspicion. How might Josephus's bias have colored his story about Eleazar in this passage?

Augustus Rises to Power

Caesar Augustus (63 B.C.E.–19 C.E.) ruled the Roman world during the birth and childhood of Jesus. The Roman historian Gaius Suetonius Tranquillus (c. 69–122 C.E.) writes here of his rise to power in Rome.

Octavius Caesar, afterwards Augustus, had now attained to the same position in the state which had formerly been occupied by Julius Caesar; and though he entered upon it by violence, he continued to enjoy it through life with almost uninterrupted tranquillity. By the long duration of the late civil war, with its concomitant train of public calamities, the minds of men were become less averse to the prospect of an absolute government; at the same time that the new emperor, naturally prudent and politic, had learned from the fate of Julius the art of preserving supreme power, without arrogating to himself any invidious mark of distinction. He affected to decline public honours, disclaimed every idea of personal superiority, and in all his behaviour displayed a degree of moderation which prognosticated the most happy effects, in restoring peace and prosperity to the harassed empire. The tenor of his future conduct was suitable to this auspicious commencement. While he endeavoured to conciliate the affections of the people by lending money to those who stood in need of it, at low interest, or without any at all, and by the exhibition of public shows, of which the Romans were remarkably fond; he was attentive to the preservation of a becoming dignity in the government, and to the correction of morals. The senate, which, in the time of Sylla, had increased to upwards of four hundred, and, during the civil war, to a thousand, members, by the admission of improper persons, he reduced to six hundred; and being invested with the ancient office of censor, which had for some time been disused, he exercised an arbitrary but legal authority over the conduct of every rank in the state; by which he could degrade senators and knights, and inflict upon all citizens an ignominious sentence for any immoral or indecent behaviour. But nothing contributed more to render the new form of government acceptable to the people, than the frequent distribution of corn, and sometimes largesses, amongst the commonalty: for an occasional scarcity of provisions had always been the chief cause of discontents and tumults in the capital. To the interests of the army he likewise paid particular attention. It was by the assistance of the legions that he had risen to power; and they were the men who, in the last resort, if such an emergency should ever occur, could alone enable him to preserve it.

Source: Suetonius, "D. Octavius Caesar Augustus" [148] in *The Lives of the Caesars,* trans. Alexander Thomson, M.D.; http://www.gutenberg.org/files/6400/6400-h/6400-h.htm

According to Suetonius, what did Augustus do to maintain his power in Rome? Do you think that Suetonius has a generally favorable or disfavorable opinion of his reign?

Questions for Group Discussion

1. Read Luke 1:1-4. How does Plutarch's explanation of biography help us better understand Luke's explanation of his biography of Jesus?
2. By the time of Jesus' public career, the Sadducees had much more political influence than the Pharisees. Who was better loved by the common people, according to Josephus? Why?
3. What seems to be Caesar Augustus's primary motivation as ruler according to Seutonius?

Questions for Reflection

1. What are other examples that illustrate the difference between the past and *accounts* of the past? How close do you think we can get to "what really happened"?

2. Most of the New Testament was composed (a) in Greek, (b) during Roman rule, (c) by first-century Jews. Which of these three factors would you say was most influential as the New Testament took shape?

11

The Gospels: Their Composition and Nature

Summary and Learning Objectives

1. The significance of Jesus' life, death, and resurrection stands at the heart of the New Testament. This story was so significant and carried so much momentum that several biographies of Jesus' public career were produced. These built upon first-century Jewish hopes for a messiah. But it was not long before Jesus' status as Messiah (or Christ) was divorced from its Jewish context. After reading this chapter (alongside chapter 11 of Sumney's text), the reader should be able *to indentify several overlaps between the Gospel of Thomas and the biblical Gospels.*
2. After reading this chapter (alongside chapter 11 of Sumney's text), the reader should be able *to explain Jesus' statements about the destruction of the Jerusalem Temple.*
3. After reading this chapter (alongside chapter 11 of Sumney's text), the reader should be able *to speak to the various messianic expectations by various groups in first-century Judaism.*

Key Terms

Dead Sea Scrolls The manuscripts found in the caves around the Qumran compound at the northwestern end of the Dead Sea. Among the scrolls were numerous commentaries on biblical books. These scrolls provide some of the earliest evidence for the form of the text of the Hebrew Bible. They also give us information about the Essenes, the movement to which the authors of the scrolls belonged.

Gospel (1) A word that means "good news." (2) Books that tell of Jesus. In the New Testament, these are narratives of Jesus' life. Some extracanonical gospels focus only on the sayings of Jesus (for example, the Gospel of Thomas). (3) The message about what Jesus accomplishes for the relationship between God and humanity, and for relations between fellow human beings.

John the Baptist   Cousin of Jesus who baptizes Jesus as he begins his ministry. John acts as the one who prepares for the ministry of Jesus in the Gospels. Some scholars think that Jesus was a follower of John before Jesus began his independent ministry.

Messiah   Anointed one. Various people throughout the Hebrew Bible were anointed, a way of appointing someone to perform specific tasks. The early church narrowed the definition of Messiah so that it designates only Jesus, the one who fulfills all proper expectations for the person God would send. To do this, they must radically redefine the tasks of the messiah.

New Testament   The collection of twenty-seven writings that the church added to the Hebrew Scriptures to complete their canon.

Key Themes

▶ The Gospels reveal a literary relationship; perhaps some of the authors used a previously written gospel in composition

▶ The Gospel of Thomas is quite unique, but not altogether different from the biblical Gospels

▶ Jewish expectations for a messiah in the first century were multiple and varied

Primary Text

Temptations in Parallel

The Gospel of Mark (composed first among the biblical Gospels) provides two short verses describing Jesus' famous temptation: "And the Spirit immediately drove him out into the wilderness. He was in the wilderness forty days, tempted by Satan; and he was with the wild beasts; and the angels waited on him" (Mark 1:12-13). The Gospel of John contains no temptation account. However, consider the similarities and differences of this account in Matthew and Luke:

[4] But he answered, "It is written, 'One does not live by bread alone, but by every word that comes from the mouth of God.' " [5] Then the devil took him to the holy city and placed him on the pinnacle of the temple, [6] saying to him, "If you are the Son of God, throw yourself down; for it is written, 'He will command his angels concerning you,' and 'On their hands they will bear you up, so that you will not dash your foot against a stone.' " [7] Jesus said to him, "Again it is written, 'Do not put the Lord your God to the test.' " [8] Again, the

[1] Jesus, full of the Holy Spirit, returned from the Jordan and was led by the Spirit in the wilderness, [2] where for forty days he was tempted by the devil. He ate nothing at all during those days, and when they were over, he was famished. [3] The devil said to him, "If you are the Son of God, command this stone to become a loaf of bread." [4] Jesus answered him, "It is written, 'One does not live by bread alone.' " [5] Then the devil led him up and showed him in an instant all the kingdoms of the world. [6] And the devil said to him, "To you I will give their glory

devil took him to a very high mountain and showed him all the kingdoms of the world and their splendor; [9] and he said to him, "All these I will give you, if you will fall down and worship me." [10] Jesus said to him, "Away with you, Satan! for it is written, 'Worship the Lord your God, and serve only him.' " [11] Then the devil left him, and suddenly angels came and waited on him. (Matthew 4:4-11)

and all this authority; for it has been given over to me, and I give it to anyone I please. [7] If you, then, will worship me, it will all be yours." [8] Jesus answered him, "It is written, 'Worship the Lord your God, and serve only him.' " [9] Then the devil took him to Jerusalem, and placed him on the pinnacle of the temple, saying to him, "If you are the Son of God, throw yourself down from here, [10] for it is written, 'He will command his angels concerning you, to protect you,' [11] and 'On their hands they will bear you up, so that you will not dash your foot against a stone.' " [12] Jesus answered him, "It is said, 'Do not put the Lord your God to the test.' " [13] When the devil had finished every test, he departed from him until an opportune time. (Luke 4:1-13)

What do the similarities in these texts suggest about their relationship? Does one copy from the other? Do they both derive from a common source? Notice the minor (but important) differences between the two. What do these differences suggest about the distinct styles of these two authors?

Jesus and the Fate of the Temple

Consider these passages from the Gospels. Each reflects some form of a historical memory about Jesus' statement about the Jerusalem temple. What is the best explanation of all of this evidence?

[1] As he came out of the temple, one of his disciples said to him, "Look, Teacher, what large stones and what large buildings!" [2] Then Jesus asked him, "Do you see these great buildings? Not one stone will be left here upon another; all will be thrown down." (Matthew 13:1-2)

[53] They took Jesus to the high priest; and all the chief priests, the elders, and the scribes were assembled. [54] Peter had followed him at a distance, right into the courtyard of the high priest; and he was sitting with the guards, warming himself at the fire. [55] Now the chief priests and the whole council were looking for testimony against Jesus to put him to death; but they found none. [56] For many gave false testimony against him, and their testimony did not agree. [57] Some stood up and gave false testimony against him, saying, [58] "We heard him say, 'I will destroy this temple that is made with hands, and in three days I will build another, not made

with hands.' " [59] But even on this point their testimony did not agree. [60] Then the high priest stood up before them and asked Jesus, "Have you no answer? What is it that they testify against you?" [61] But he was silent and did not answer . . . (Mark 14:53-61)

[19] Jesus answered them, "Destroy this temple, and in three days I will raise it up." [20] The Jews then said, "This temple has been under construction for forty-six years, and will you raise it up in three days?" [21] But he was speaking of the temple of his body. [22] After he was raised from the dead, his disciples remembered that he had said this; and they believed the scripture and the word that Jesus had spoken. (John 2:19-22)

Did Jesus claim to be able to destroy the temple? Did he claim to rebuild it? Did he claim that it would be destroyed, but not by him? Did he claim nothing about the literal temple, but rather claim something about his own body? Which of these solutions gives us the best understanding of Jesus?

The Gospel of Thomas

The four biblical Gospels have a great deal in common. The Gospel of John seems to be distinct in many ways, but it is not difficult to find many more similarities. Thomas (not included in the New Testament) represents a gospel that is significantly different from the four-fold Gospel tradition. While Thomas post-dates the first century, it may preserve some content from the first century. There are a total of 114 sayings in Thomas (with very little narration). I have only included a selection of these sayings here. Look for parallels with New Testament tradition as well as unique content.

[2] Jesus said, "Those who seek should not stop seeking until they find. When they find, they will be disturbed. When they are disturbed, they will marvel, and will reign over all. [And after they have reigned they will rest.]"

[8] And he said, The person is like a wise fisherman who cast his net into the sea and drew it up from the sea full of little fish. Among them the wise fisherman discovered a fine large fish. He threw all the little fish back into the sea, and easily chose the large fish. Anyone here with two good ears had better listen!

[9] Jesus said, Look, the sower went out, took a handful (of seeds), and scattered (them). Some fell on the road, and the birds came and gathered them. Others fell on rock, and they didn't take root in the soil and didn't produce heads of grain. Others fell on thorns, and they choked the seeds and worms ate them. And others fell on good soil, and it produced a good crop: it yielded sixty per measure and one hundred twenty per measure.

[11] Jesus said, "This heaven will pass away, and the one above it will pass away.

The dead are not alive, and the living will not die. During the days when you ate what is dead, you made it come alive. When you are in the light, what will you do? On the day when you were one, you became two. But when you become two, what will you do?"

[16] Jesus said, "Perhaps people think that I have come to easy peace upon the world. They do not know that I have come to cast conflicts upon the earth: fire, sword, war.

For there will be five in a house: there'll be three against two and two against three, father against son and son against father, and they will stand alone."

[20] The disciples said to Jesus, "Tell us what Heaven's kingdom is like."

He said to them, It's like a mustard seed, the smallest of all seeds, but when it falls on prepared soil, it produces a large plant and becomes a shelter for birds of the sky.

[25] Jesus said, "Love your friends like your own soul, protect them like the pupil of your eye."

[26] Jesus said, "You see the sliver in your friend's eye, but you don't see the timber in your own eye. When you take the timber out of your own eye, then you will see well enough to remove the sliver from your friend's eye."

[31] Jesus said, "No prophet is welcome on his home turf; doctors don't cure those who know them."

[35] Jesus said, "One can't enter a strong person's house and take it by force without tying his hands. Then one can loot his house."

[36] Jesus said, "Do not fret, from morning to evening and from evening to morning, [about your food—what you're going to eat, or about your clothing—] what you are going to wear. [You're much better than the lilies, which neither card nor spin.

As for you, when you have no garment, what will you put on? Who might add to your stature? That very one will give you your garment.]"

[44] Jesus said, "Whoever blasphemes against the Father will be forgiven, and whoever blasphemes against the son will be forgiven, but whoever blasphemes against the holy spirit will not be forgiven, either on earth or in heaven."

[46] Jesus said, "From Adam to John the Baptist, among those born of women, no one is so much greater than John the Baptist that his eyes should not be averted.

But I have said that whoever among you becomes a child will recognize the kingdom and will become greater than John."

[47] Jesus said, "A person cannot mount two horses or bend two bows. And a slave cannot serve two masters, otherwise that slave will honor the one and offend the other.

"Nobody drinks aged wine and immediately wants to drink young wine. Young wine is not poured into old wineskins, or they might break, and aged wine is not poured into a new wineskin, or it might spoil. An old patch is not sewn onto a new garment, since it would create a tear."

[61] Jesus said, "Two will recline on a couch; one will die, one will live."

Salome said, "Who are you mister? You have climbed onto my couch and eaten from my table as if you are from someone."

Jesus said to her, "I am the one who comes from what is whole. I was granted from the things of my Father."

"I am your disciple."

"For this reason I say, if one is whole, one will be filled with light, but if one is divided, one will be filled with darkness."

⁶⁵ He said, A [. . .] person owned a vineyard and rented it to some farmers, so they could work it and he could collect its crop from them. He sent his slave so the farmers would give him the vineyard's crop. They grabbed him, beat him, and almost killed him, and the slave returned and told his master. His master said, "Perhaps he didn't know them." He sent another slave, and the farmers beat that one as well. Then the master sent his son and said, "Perhaps they'll show my son some respect." Because the farmers knew that he was the heir to the vineyard, they grabbed him and killed him. Anyone here with two ears had better listen!

⁶⁶ Jesus said, "Show me the stone that the builders rejected: that is the keystone."

⁷⁷ Jesus said, "I am the light that is over all things. I am all: from me all came forth, and to me all attained.

Split a piece of wood; I am there.

Lift up the stone, and you will find me there."

⁷⁹ A woman in the crowd said to him, "Lucky are the womb that bore you and the breasts that fed you."

He said to [her], "Lucky are those who have heard the word of the Father and have truly kept it. For there will be days when you will say, 'Lucky are the womb that has not conceived and the breasts that have not given milk.' "

⁹⁰ Jesus said, "Come to me, for my yoke is comfortable and my lordship is gentle, and you will find rest for yourselves."

⁹⁴ Jesus [said], "One who seeks will find, and for [one who knocks] it will be opened."

⁹⁵ [Jesus said], "If you have money, don't lend it at interest. Rather, give [it] to someone from whom you won't get it back."

¹⁰⁰ They showed Jesus a gold coin and said to him, "The Roman emperor's people demand taxes from us."

He said to them, "Give the emperor what belongs to the emperor, give God what belongs to God, and give me what is mine."

¹⁰¹ "Whoever does not hate [father] and mother as I do cannot be my [disciple], and whoever does [not] love [father and] mother as I do cannot be my [disciple]. For my mother [. . .], but my true [mother] gave me life."

¹⁰² Jesus said, "Damn the Pharisees! They are like a dog sleeping in the cattle manger: the dog neither eats nor [lets] the cattle eat."

¹⁰⁹ Jesus said, The (Father's) kingdom is like a person who had a treasure hidden in his field but did not know it. And [when] he died he left it to his [son]. The son [did] not know about it either. He took over the field and sold it. The buyer went plowing, [discovered] the treasure, and began to lend money at interest to whomever he wished.

Source: Stephen Patterson and Marvin Meyer, *The Complete Gospels: Annotated Scholars Version* (Santa Rosa: Polebridge Press, 1994); http://www.earlychristianwritings.com/text/thomas-scholars.html

Jewish Messianism at the Time of Jesus

Matthew 11:4-5 (compare with Luke 7:21-22) puts forth an exchange between Jesus and the followers of John the Baptist. John wants to know if Jesus is the "one who is to come." Jesus' reply includes a quotation from Isaiah 61:1-2. "Jesus answered them, 'Go and tell John what you hear and see: the blind receive their sight, the lame walk, the lepers are cleansed, the deaf hear, the dead are raised, and the poor have good news brought to them.' " A passage from the Dead Sea Scrolls uses the same passage from Isaiah to build messianic expectation (elsewhere this group promotes the idea of multiple messiahs). Keep in mind that the word "messiah" literally means "anointed one." This fragmentary text reads:

> [. . . for the heav]ens and the earth will listen to his anointed one, [and all] that is in them will not turn away from the precepts of the holy ones. Strengthen yourselves, you who are seeking the Lord, in his service! Will you not in this encounter the Lord, all those who hope in their heart? For the Lord will consider the pious and call the righteous by name, and his spirit will hover upon the poor, and he will renew the faithful with his strength. For he will honor the pious upon the throne of an eternal kingdom, freeing prisoners, giving sight to the blind, straightening out the twis[ted.] And for[e]ver shall I cling to [those who] hope, and in his mercy [. . .] and the fru[it of . . .] not be delayed. And the Lord will perform marvelous acts such as have not existed, just as he sa[id, for] he will heal the badly wounded and will make the dead live; he will proclaim good news to the poor and [. . .] he will lead the [. . .] and enrich the hungry. [. . .] and all [. . . .]

Source: Florentino García Martínez and Eibert J. C. Tigschelaar, trans. and ed., *The Dead Sea Scrolls: Study Edition* (Grand Rapids: Eerdmans 2000), 1044–47.

Questions for Group Discussion

1. Given that Thomas post-dates the biblical Gospels, do you think it derives from a similar source?
2. How is the tone of Jesus represented differently in the Thomas?
3. What it Jesus' relationship with the Jerusalem temple?

Questions for Reflection

1. Why do you think John the Baptist questioned Jesus' status?

2. How do you think the temptation account came to be written down?

12

Four Views of One Jesus: Mark, Matthew, Luke, and John

Summary and Learning Objectives

1. The biblical Gospels present four different but overlapping portraits of Jesus. They all use similar titles for Jesus and interpret his significance, death, and resurrection in similar ways. They also reveal different (sometimes competing) interpretations about Jesus' significance among first-century Jews. After reading this chapter (alongside chapter 12 of Sumney's text), the reader should be able *to identify a few differences in the literary styles of the various gospel writers.*
2. After reading this chapter (alongside chapter 12 of Sumney's text), the reader should be able *to speak to the belief of demons in the first century.*
3. After reading this chapter (alongside chapter 12 of Sumney's text), the reader should be able *to identify a few differences between the Pharisees and the Sadducees.*
4. After reading this chapter (alongside chapter 12 of Sumney's text), the reader should be able *to explain at least two different perspectives on the supernatural in the first century.*

Key Terms

Exorcism Getting a demon out of a person.

Kingdom of heaven Matthew's way of referring to the kingdom of God. This expression shows Matthew's Jewish sensibilities because he is avoiding direct mention of God.

Pharisees One of the leading sects of Judaism in the first century C.E. They were known as the expert interpreters of the Law.

Sadducees One of the leading sects of Judaism in the first century C.E. This group had many priests as members.

Synoptic Gospels Designation for Matthew, Mark, and Luke, given because they are alike in so many ways. The Synoptic problem is the question of how these Gospels are related to one another. Most interpreters think they have some literary relationship.

Key Themes

▶ Both in word and deed, Jesus is presented as a mysterious figure in the Gospels

▶ Some of what Jesus does and says is better understood by understanding the world in which he lived

▶ Each gospel writer changes the stories about Jesus to make better sense of them from their point of view

Primary Text

Parables

In Mark 4:10-12, Jesus talks about the reason he speaks in parables in a way that sounds strange to us. But the very nature of parables means that hearers must figure out what they mean. Jesus was not the only teacher who used parables in that time. Compare the following parable from the Testament of Job to those in Matthew 13:44-50. The passage in the Testament of Job (first century B.C.E. to first century C.E.) has Job recall his reactions to the terrible things that have happened to his family, but also remembering promises that God had given him.

And I became as one wishing to enter a certain city to discover its wealth and gain a portion of its splendor, and as one embarked with cargo in a seagoing ship. Seeing at mid-ocean the third wave and the opposition of the wind, he threw the cargo into the sea, saying, "I am willing to lose everything in order to enter this city so that I might gain both the ship and things better than the payload. Thus, I also considered my goods as nothing compared to the city about which the angel spoke to me."

Source: R. P. Spittler, trans., Testament of Job 18:6-8 in *The Old Testament Pseudepigrapha: Apocalyptic Literature and Testaments,* ed. James H. Charlesworth (Garden City, New York: Doubleday, 1983).

Notice that this writer provides the meaning, something Jesus seldom does in the Gospels. Why do you think the Gospels do not have Jesus reveal the correct meaning of his parables?

The Beatitudes

One of group of sayings that take on different shapes in Matthew and Luke is what we called the "Beatitudes." In Matthew this is the Sermon on the Mount; in Luke this is the Sermon on the Plain. Beyond the location difference, notice the change in content in these passages:

Why does Matthew use the phrase "kingdom of heaven," while Luke uses "kingdom of God"? What

[1] When Jesus saw the crowds, he went up the mountain; and after he sat down, his disciples came to him. [2] Then he began to speak, and taught them, saying:

[3] "Blessed are the poor in spirit, for theirs is the kingdom of heaven.

[4] "Blessed are those who mourn, for they will be comforted.

[5] "Blessed are the meek, for they will inherit the earth.

[6] "Blessed are those who hunger and thirst for righteousness, for they will be filled.

[7] "Blessed are the merciful, for they will receive mercy.

[8] "Blessed are the pure in heart, for they will see God.

[9] "Blessed are the peacemakers, for they will be called children of God.

[10] "Blessed are those who are persecuted for righteousness' sake, for theirs is the kingdom of heaven.

[11] "Blessed are you when people revile you and persecute you and utter all kinds of evil against you falsely on my account. [12] Rejoice and be glad, for your reward is great in heaven, for in the same way they persecuted the prophets who were before you. (Matthew 5:1-12)

[17] He came down with them and stood on a level place, with a great crowd of his disciples and a great multitude of people from all Judea, Jerusalem, and the coast of Tyre and Sidon. [18] They had come to hear him and to be healed of their diseases; and those who were troubled with unclean spirits were cured. [19] And all in the crowd were trying to touch him, for power came out from him and healed all of them.

[20] Then he looked up at his disciples and said:

"Blessed are you who are poor,
    for yours is the kingdom of God.
[21] "Blessed are you who are hungry now,
    for you will be filled.
"Blessed are you who weep now,
    for you will laugh.

[22] "Blessed are you when people hate you, and when they exclude you, revile you, and defame you on account of the Son of Man. [23] Rejoice in that day and leap for joy, for surely your reward is great in heaven; for that is what their ancestors did to the prophets.

[24] "But woe to you who are rich,
    for you have received your consolation.
[25] "Woe to you who are full now,
    for you will be hungry.
"Woe to you who are laughing now,
    for you will mourn and weep.

26 "Woe to you when all speak well of you, for that is what their ancestors did to the false prophets (Luke 6:17-26)

is the socio-economic group targeted in Luke's version? What are some other similarities and differences in these two passages?

Casting out Demons

One of the things that separates Jesus from his contemporaries is the informality of his exorcisms. Other exorcists during this period used charms, bowls, roots, and (in many cases) specific incantations. A few fragmentary psalms found among the Dead Sea Scrolls seem to have been used to cast out demons. In these psalms, the names of Solomon and David were used to wield power over the demonic realm. In the below passage, this "psalm of David" was used against a powerful demon named "Resheph." Notice the mocking tone used against this demon:

> A Psalm of David, against [. . .] in the name of the Lor[d . . .] against Resheph [. . .] he will come to you at ni[ght, and] you will say to him, "Who are you? [Withdraw from] humanity and from the ho[ly] race! For your appearance is [nothing], and your horns are horns of sand. You are darkness, not light, [wicked]ness, not righteousness [. . .] the Lord [. . . in Had]es most deep, [enclosed in doors] of bronze [. . .] light and not [. . . never again to see] the sun that [shines on the] righteous [. . .] and then you shall say [. . .] the righteous to come [. . .] to do harm to him [. . . tr]uth from [. . . righ]teousness to [. . .]"

Source: 11Q11 Col. IV in M. Wise, M. Abegg, and E. Cook, eds., *The Dead Sea Scrolls: A New Translation* (San Francisco: HarperSanFrancisco, 1996), 454.

Compare this psalm with this account of Jesus' exorcism in Matthew:

[22] Then they brought to him a demoniac who was blind and mute; and he cured him, so that the one who had been mute could speak and see. [23] All the crowds were amazed and said, "Can this be the Son of David?" [24] But when the Pharisees heard it, they said, "It is only by Beelzebul, the ruler of the demons, that this fellow casts out the demons." [25] He knew what they were thinking and said to them, "Every kingdom divided against itself is laid waste, and no city or house divided against itself will stand. [26] If Satan casts out Satan, he is divided against himself; how then will his kingdom stand? [27] If I cast out demons by Beelzebul, by whom do your own exorcists cast them out? Therefore they will be your judges. [28] But if it is by the Spirit of God that I cast out demons, then the kingdom of God has come to you. [29] Or how can one enter a strong man's house and plunder his property, without first tying up the strong man? Then indeed the house can be plundered. [30] Whoever is not with me is against me, and whoever does not gather with me scatters. [31] Therefore I tell you, people will be forgiven for every sin and blasphemy, but blasphemy against the Spirit will not be forgiven. [32] Whoever speaks a word against the Son of Man will be forgiven, but whoever speaks against the Holy Spirit will not be forgiven, either in this age or in the age to come. (Matthew 12:22-32)

Why do you think that David, or the "son of David" (presumably, Solomon) were thought to have power over the demonic realm during this period?

The Beliefs of the Pharisees and Sadducees

The first-century group to which Jesus has much in common is the Pharisees. The commonalities between Jesus and the Pharisees far exceed their differences. This explains why they become Jesus' chief conversation and debate partners in the Gospels. While they become antagonists in these narratives, we should not assume that they were historical enemies of Jesus or Christianity. Josephus writes of their beliefs:

> [12] Now, for the Pharisees, they live meanly, and despise delicacies in diet; and they follow the conduct of reason; and what that prescribes to them as good for them they do; and they think they ought earnestly to strive to observe reason's dictates for practice. They also pay a respect to such as are in years; nor are they so bold as to contradict them in any thing which they have introduced; [13] and when they determine that all things are done by fate, they do not take away the freedom from men of acting as they think fit; since their notion is, that it hath pleased God to make a temperament, whereby what he wills is done, but so that the will of man can act virtuously or viciously. [14] They also believe that souls have an immortal rigor in them, and that under the earth there will be rewards or punishments, according as they have lived virtuously or viciously in this life; and the latter are to be detained in an everlasting prison, but that the former shall have power to revive and live again; [15] on account of which doctrines they are able greatly to persuade the body of the people; and whatsoever they do about divine worship, prayers, and sacrifices, they perform them according to their direction; insomuch that the cities give great attestations to them on account of their entire virtuous conduct, both in the actions of their lives and their discourses also. (*Ant* 18.12-15)

Source: William Whiston, trans., *The Works of Flavius Josephus* (Worcester: Isaiah Thomas, 1793)

The Sadducees seem to have enjoyed great political influence in Jerusalem. Jesus probably did not have much interaction with the Sadducees while in Galilee. He does seem to have gotten into trouble with the Jerusalem temple establishment (including the Sadducees) shortly before his death. Josephus describes them this way:

> [16] But the doctrine of the Sadducees is this: That souls die with the bodies; nor do they regard the observation of anything besides what the law enjoins them; for they think it an instance of virtue to dispute with those teachers of philosophy whom they frequent: [17] but this doctrine is received but by a few, yet by those still of the greatest dignity. But they are able to do almost nothing of themselves; for when they become magistrates, as they are unwillingly and by force sometimes obliged to be, they addict themselves to the notions of the Pharisees, because the multitude would not otherwise bear them. (*Ant* 18.16-17)

Source: William Whiston, trans., *The Works of Flavius Josephus* (Worcester: Isaiah Thomas, 1737)

Raising the Dead

A Greek teacher named Apollonius of Tyana (c. 15–100 C.E.) gained a reputation for healing shortly after the time of Jesus. Philostratus (much like a gospel author) writes a defense against what he believed to be unwarranted slander of Apollonius. The author also, on occasion, attempts to rationalize the seemingly supernatural healings of Apollonius. In one episode, the healer raises a girl from the dead. But Philostratus's commentary betrays his doubt of the supernatural:

> Now whether he detected some spark of life in her, which those who were nursing her had not noticed (for it is said that although it was raining at the time, a vapor went up from her face) or whether her life was really extinct, and he restored it by the warmth of his touch, is a mysterious problem which neither I myself nor those who were present could decide. (4.45)
>
> Source: Philostratus, *Life of Apollonius of Tyana*, trans. F. C. Conybeare, Loeb Classics Library 16, 17 (London: Macmillan, 1912).

It is important to recognize that the author is sincerely attempting to make sense of the story for himself. This suggests that some ancient people had a different perspective on the supernatural. Could this explain why the Gospel of John does not contain any stories of exorcism?

Jesus and Samaritans

Jews and Samaritans were enemies, even though they were ethnically related. Josephus gives us a hint about how he thinks of Samaritans in the following description of their behavior in the time of Antiochus.

257 When the Samaritans saw the Jews under these sufferings, they no longer confessed that they were of their kindred, nor that the temple on Mount Gerizzim belonged to Almighty God. This was according to their nature, as we have already shown. And they now said that they were a colony of Medes and Persians; and indeed they were a colony of theirs. 258 So they sent ambassadors to Antiochus, and an epistle, whose contents are these: "To king Antiochus the god, Epiphanes, a memorial from the Sidonians, who live at Shechem . . ." (*Ant.* 12.257.5–258)

Source: William Whiston, trans., *The Works of Flavius Josephus* (Worcester: Isaiah Thomas, 1737)

Now take a look at this story from the Gospel of John.

1 Now when Jesus learned that the Pharisees had heard, "Jesus is making and baptizing more disciples than John" 2—although it was not Jesus himself but his disciples who baptized— 3 he left Judea and started back to Galilee.

4 But he had to go through Samaria. 5 So he came to a Samaritan city called Sychar, near the plot of ground that Jacob had given to his son Joseph. 6 Jacob's well was there, and Jesus, tired out by his journey, was sitting by the well. It was about noon. 7 A Samaritan woman came to draw water, and Jesus said to her, "Give me a drink." 8 (His disciples had gone to the city to buy food.) 9 The Samaritan woman said to him, "How is it that you, a Jew, ask a drink of me, a woman of Samaria?" (Jews do not

share things in common with Samaritans.) [10] Jesus answered her, "If you knew the gift of God, and who it is that is saying to you, 'Give me a drink,' you would have asked him, and he would have given you living water." [11] The woman said to him, "Sir, you have no bucket, and the well is deep. Where do you get that living water? [12] Are you greater than our ancestor Jacob, who gave us the well, and with his sons and his flocks drank from it?" [13] Jesus said to her, "Everyone who drinks of this water will be thirsty again, [14] but those who drink of the water that I will give them will never be thirsty. The water that I will give will become in them a spring of water gushing up to eternal life." [15] The woman said to him, "Sir, give me this water, so that I may never be thirsty or have to keep coming here to draw water." [16] Jesus said to her, "Go, call your husband, and come back." [17] The woman answered him, "I have no husband." Jesus said to her, "You are right in saying, 'I have no husband'; [18] for you have had five husbands, and the one you have now is not your husband. What you have said is true!" [19] The woman said to him, "Sir, I see that you are a prophet. [20] Our ancestors worshiped on this mountain, but you say that the place where people must worship is in Jerusalem." [21] Jesus said to her, "Woman, believe me, the hour is coming when you will worship the Father neither on this mountain nor in Jerusalem. [22] You worship what you do not know; we worship what we know, for salvation is from the Jews. [23] But the hour is coming, and is now here, when the true worshipers will worship the Father in spirit and truth, for the Father seeks such as these to worship him. [24] God is spirit, and those who worship him must worship in spirit and truth." [25] The woman said to him, "I know that Messiah is coming" (who is called Christ). "When he comes, he will proclaim all things to us." [26] Jesus said to her, "I am he, the one who is speaking to you."

[27] Just then his disciples came. They were astonished that he was speaking with a woman, but no one said, "What do you want?" or, "Why are you speaking with her?" [28] Then the woman left her water jar and went back to the city. She said to the people, [29] "Come and see a man who told me everything I have ever done! He cannot be the Messiah, can he?" [30] They left the city and were on their way to him. [31] Meanwhile the disciples were urging him, "Rabbi, eat something." [32] But he said to them, "I have food to eat that you do not know about." [33] So the disciples said to one another, "Surely no one has brought him something to eat?" [34] Jesus said to them, "My food is to do the will of him who sent me and to complete his work. [35] Do you not say, 'Four months more, then comes the harvest'? But I tell you, look around you, and see how the fields are ripe for harvesting. [36] The reaper is already receiving wages and is gathering fruit for eternal life, so that sower and reaper may rejoice together. [37] For here the saying holds true, 'One sows and another reaps.' [38] I sent you to reap that for which you did not labor. Others have labored, and you have entered into their labor." [39] Many Samaritans from that city believed

in him because of the woman's testimony, "He told me everything I have ever done." [40] So when the Samaritans came to him, they asked him to stay with them; and he stayed there two days. [41] And many more believed because of his word. [42] They said to the woman, "It is no longer because of what you said that we believe, for we have heard for ourselves, and we know that this is truly the Savior of the world." (John 4:1-42)

What does this story suggest about Jesus' view of "insiders" and "outsiders"? What does this suggest about Jesus' view of social conventions?

Questions for Group Discussion

1. Why is Matthew's account of the "beatitudes" so different from Luke's?
2. Why is Jesus called "the son of David" in Matthew 12 after he casts out a demon?
3. What are a few ideological differences between the Pharisees and Sadducees?

Questions for Reflection

1. The Hebrew Bible tells almost no stories of exorcism. Why are there so many of these episodes in Matthew, Mark, and Luke?

2. The Gospel of John tells no stories of exorcism. What accounts for this difference between John and the Synoptics?

13

The Story Continues: The Acts of the Apostles

Summary and Learning Objectives

1. The story of Acts is a sequel to the Gospel of Luke. It explains how Jesus' resurrection and promise of the Holy Spirit motivated his followers to preach, perform powerful acts, and grow in amazing ways. It also introduces one of the most important figures of emerging Christianity: the apostle Paul. After reading this chapter (alongside chapter 13 of Sumney's text), the reader should be able *to identify several parallels between episodes between the Hebrew Bible and Acts.*

2. After reading this chapter (alongside chapter 13 of Sumney's text), the reader should be able *to speak to various first-century hopes for the coming of a "holy spirit."*

3. After reading this chapter (alongside chapter 13 of Sumney's text), the reader should be able *to better explain the purpose of the story of the deaths of Ananias and Sapphira.*

4. After reading this chapter (alongside chapter 13 of Sumney's text), the reader should be able *to compare and contrast the trials of Stephen and Jesus.*

5. After reading this chapter (alongside chapter 13 of Sumney's text), the reader should be able *to relate the character of Nero to the first-century political climate in Rome.*

Key Terms

Apostle   Most generally it means one who is sent. In the early church it comes to designate those who are recognized as the authorities in the church, particularly the Twelve (after they replace Judas), James, the brother of Jesus who becomes the leader of the Jerusalem church, and Paul. Others could be apostles in the sense that they were sent on missions by their churches, but these fourteen people were seen as sent by Christ and so as authoritative.

Ark of the Covenant   Ornate box that symbolized the presence of God. It contained relics symbolic of particular divine acts (the tablets of the law, Aaron's rod that bloomed, and a pot of manna).

Babel A place where Genesis says the people tried to build a tower to heaven. God responds by multiplying the languages the people speak so they are not able to understand one another. Thus they must abandon their project.

Barnabas Early member of the Jerusalem church who becomes a missionary of the church in Antioch. From there he recruits Paul to be a missionary with him and they travel together in southeastern Asia Minor (Turkey), establishing churches that are made up primarily of gentiles.

Nero Roman emperor who reigned 37–68 C.E. He accused the church of setting the fire that damaged much of the city of Rome in 64 C.E. This may be the first time that the Roman government officially identified members of the church as a group that was something other than simply a sect within Judaism.

Purity (ritual or cultic) The state of readiness to enter the presence of God. Its opposite is being unclean.

Key Themes

- Acts conveys the sense of a new world order, including troubling unrest and hope for renewal
- The hope for spiritual renewal is in some ways similar to the hopes held by the Dead Sea community
- Acts sets the new "church" against several adversaries, including the Jerusalem and Roman elite

Primary Text

A Holy Spirit

In the first chapter of Acts, the author addresses his reader, speaks to his purpose in writing, offers a summary of the Gospel of Luke (the first volume of this two-part work), and conveys one last dialogue between Jesus and his disciples.

[1] In the first book, Theophilus, I wrote about all that Jesus did and taught from the beginning [2] until the day when he was taken up to heaven, after giving instructions through the Holy Spirit to the apostles whom he had chosen. [3] After his suffering he presented himself alive to them by many convincing proofs, appearing to them during forty days and speaking about the kingdom of God. [4] While staying with them, he ordered them not to leave Jerusalem, but to wait there for the promise of the Father. "This," he said, "is what you have heard from me; [5] for John baptized with water, but you will be baptized with the Holy Spirit not many days from now."

[6] So when they had come together, they asked him, "Lord, is this the time when you will restore the kingdom to Israel?" [7] He replied, "It is not for you to know the times or periods that the Father has set by his own authority. [8] But you will receive power when the Holy Spirit has come upon you; and you will be my witnesses in Jerusalem, in all Judea and Samaria, and to the ends of the earth." (Acts 1:1-8)

The author of Acts believes that apostles (those sent) of Jesus now waiting for the imminent arrival of the "Holy Spirit." The promise of this Holy Spirit answers the question ask by the disciples, "Lord, is this the time when you will restore the kingdom to Israel?" (Acts 1:6) The group that collected and wrote the Dead Sea Scrolls also hoped for a restoration of Israel and hoped for the imminent arrival of a "holy spirit." Look for other similarities between this group and the book of Acts:

> [God] allotted unto humanity two spirits that he should walk in them until the time of His visitation; they are the spirits of truth and perversity. The origin of truth is in a fountain of light, and the origin of perversity is from a fountain of darkness. Dominion over all the sons of righteousness is in the hand of the Prince of light; they walk in the ways of light. All dominion over the sons of perversity is in the hand of the Angel of darkness; they walk in the ways of darkness . . . (1QS 3:18-21).

> In his mysterious insight and glorious wisdom God has countenanced an era in which perversity triumphs, but at the appointed time for visitation He shall destroy such forever. Then shall truth come forth in victory upon the earth. Sullied by wicked ways while perversity rules, at the time of the appointed judgment truth shall be decreed. By His truth God shall then purify all human deeds by a holy spirit. Like purifying waters, He shall sprinkle each with a spirit of truth, effectual against all abominations of lying and sullying by an unclean spirit. Thereby He shall give the upright insight into the knowledge of the Most High and the wisdom of angels, making wise those following the perfect way . . . (1QS 4:18-22)

Source: M. Wise, M. Abegg, and E. Cook, eds., *The Dead Sea Scrolls: A New Translation* (San Francisco: HarperSanFrancisco, 1996), 130–131.

It might be interesting to note that this Dead Sea community called themselves "the way" (compare with Acts 9:2), compared purification by water to that of a holy spirit (compare with Acts 1:5), and hoped for a restored Jerusalem temple in the last days. In these ways and more, these groups had a great deal in common.

Common Tongues

Genesis 11:1-9 tells a story meant to explain why there are so many different and unintelligible languages in the world:

> [1] Now the whole earth had one language and the same words. [2] And as they migrated from the east, they came upon a plain in the land of Shinar and settled there. [3] And they said to one another, "Come, let us make bricks, and burn them thoroughly." And they had brick for stone, and bitumen for mortar. [4] Then they said, "Come, let us build ourselves a city, and a tower with its top in the heavens, and let us make a name for ourselves; otherwise we shall be scattered abroad upon the face of the whole earth."
> [5] The Lord came down to see the city and the tower, which mortals had built. [6] And the Lord said, "Look, they are one people, and they have all one language; and this is only the beginning of what they will do; nothing that they propose to do will now be impossible for them. [7] Come, let us go down, and confuse their language there, so that they will not understand one

another's speech." ⁸ So the Lord scattered them abroad from there over the face of all the earth, and they left off building the city. ⁹ Therefore it was called Babel, because there the Lord confused the language of all the earth; and from there the Lord scattered them abroad over the face of all the earth. (Genesis 11:1-9)

Compare this story with Acts 2:1-12:

¹ When the day of Pentecost had come, they were all together in one place. ² And suddenly from heaven there came a sound like the rush of a violent wind, and it filled the entire house where they were sitting. ³ Divided tongues, as of fire, appeared among them, and a tongue rested on each of them. ⁴ All of them were filled with the Holy Spirit and began to speak in other languages, as the Spirit gave them ability.

⁵ Now there were devout Jews from every nation under heaven living in Jerusalem. ⁶ And at this sound the crowd gathered and was bewildered, because each one heard them speaking in the native language of each. ⁷ Amazed and astonished, they asked, "Are not all these who are speaking Galileans? ⁸ And how is it that we hear, each of us, in our own native language? ⁹ Parthians, Medes, Elamites, and residents of Mesopotamia, Judea and Cappadocia, Pontus and Asia, ¹⁰ Phrygia and Pamphylia, Egypt and the parts of Libya belonging to Cyrene, and visitors from Rome, both Jews and proselytes, ¹¹ Cretans and Arabs—in our own languages we hear them speaking about God's deeds of power." ¹² All

were amazed and perplexed, saying to one another, "What does this mean?"

How do these stories relate? Is the story in Acts a solution to the specific problem described in Genesis?

The Peril of the Lord's Temple Presence

While there is a great deal of violence in the Bible, it is quite rare that the Lord is the direct source of summary execution. When these two criteria are employed—instantly and directly killed by God—such violence happens exclusively in proximity to the Lord's Ark of the Covenant presence (most associated with the Holy of Holies in the Temple). These examples include Nadab and Abihu (Leviticus 10:1-2), the sons of Korah (Numbers 16:31-35), the sons of Eli (1 Samuel 2), the seventy Israelites who look upon the Ark (1 Samuel 6), and Uzzah (2 Samuel 6:6-7). Take a look at the first of these examples:

¹ Now Aaron's sons, Nadab and Abihu, each took his censer, put fire in it, and laid incense on it; and they offered unholy fire before the Lord, such as he had not commanded them. ² And fire came out from the presence of the Lord and consumed them, and they died before the Lord. (Leviticus 10:1-2)

Now consider the story of Barnabus, Ananias, and Sapphira. Keep in mind that these early Christians are congregated in the Jerusalem temple:

³² Now the whole group of those who believed were of one heart and soul, and no one claimed private ownership of any possessions, but everything they owned was held in common. ³³ With great power the apostles gave their testimony to the

resurrection of the Lord Jesus, and great grace was upon them all. [34] There was not a needy person among them, for as many as owned lands or houses sold them and brought the proceeds of what was sold. [35] They laid it at the apostles' feet, and it was distributed to each as any had need. [36] There was a Levite, a native of Cyprus, Joseph, to whom the apostles gave the name Barnabas (which means "son of encouragement"). [37] He sold a field that belonged to him, then brought the money, and laid it at the apostles' feet.

5 [1] But a man named Ananias, with the consent of his wife Sapphira, sold a piece of property; [2] with his wife's knowledge, he kept back some of the proceeds, and brought only a part and laid it at the apostles' feet. [3] "Ananias," Peter asked, "why has Satan filled your heart to lie to the Holy Spirit and to keep back part of the proceeds of the land? [4] While it remained unsold, did it not remain your own? And after it was sold, were not the proceeds at your disposal? How is it that you have contrived this deed in your heart? You did not lie to us but to God!" [5] Now when Ananias heard these words, he fell down and died. And great fear seized all who heard of it. [6] The young men came and wrapped up his body, then carried him out and buried him. [7] After an interval of about three hours his wife came in, not knowing what had happened. [8] Peter said to her, "Tell me whether you and your husband sold the land for such and such a price." And she said, "Yes, that was the price." [9] Then Peter said to her, "How is it that you have agreed together to

put the Spirit of the Lord to the test? Look, the feet of those who have buried your husband are at the door, and they will carry you out." [10] Immediately she fell down at his feet and died. When the young men came in they found her dead, so they carried her out and buried her beside her husband. [11] And great fear seized the whole church and all who heard of these things.

[12] Now many signs and wonders were done among the people through the apostles. And they were all together in Solomon's Portico. (Acts 4:32—5:12)

The author of Acts conveys that the apostles and their followers have become the economic, social, and worshiping center of Jerusalem. Peter acts analogously to the Holy of Holies or the Ark in these stories from the Hebrew Bible. In all of these ways, their group is functioning like the Jerusalem temple. Given this, what is the purpose of the story of the summary executions of Ananias and Sapphira? What message does this send to the reader of Acts?

Vindicating Martyrs

The early Christians believed that they were persecuted for demonstrating their power in Christ in public. While many question how much persecution came from their Jewish kinsmen, the Gospels and Acts place the blame firmly on the Jerusalem temple establishment. Notice the points of similarity between Mark's account of Jesus' trial and the account of Stephen's trial in Acts:

[53] They took Jesus to the high priest; and all the chief priests, the elders, and the scribes were assembled. [54] Peter had followed him at a distance, right into the courtyard of the high priest; and he was sitting with the

guards, warming himself at the fire. ⁵⁵ Now the chief priests and the whole council were looking for testimony against Jesus to put him to death; but they found none. ⁵⁶ For many gave false testimony against him, and their testimony did not agree. ⁵⁷ Some stood up and gave false testimony against him, saying, ⁵⁸ "We heard him say, 'I will destroy this temple that is made with hands, and in three days I will build another, not made with hands.' " ⁵⁹ But even on this point their testimony did not agree. ⁶⁰ Then the high priest stood up before them and asked Jesus, "Have you no answer? What is it that they testify against you?" ⁶¹ But he was silent and did not answer. Again the high priest asked him, "Are you the Messiah, the Son of the Blessed One?" ⁶² Jesus said, "I am; and

> 'you will see the Son of Man
> seated at the right hand of the Power,'
> and 'coming with the clouds of heaven.' "

⁶³ Then the high priest tore his clothes and said, "Why do we still need witnesses? ⁶⁴ You have heard his blasphemy! What is your decision?" All of them condemned him as deserving death. ⁶⁵ Some began to spit on him, to blindfold him, and to strike him, saying to him, "Prophesy!" The guards also took him over and beat him.

⁶⁶ While Peter was below in the courtyard, one of the servant-girls of the high priest came by. ⁶⁷ When she saw Peter warming himself, she stared at him and said, "You also were with Jesus, the man from Nazareth."⁶⁸ But he denied it, saying, "I do not know or understand what you are talking about." And he went out into the forecourt. Then the cock crowed. ⁶⁹ And the servant-girl, on seeing him, began again to say to the bystanders, "This man is one of them." ⁷⁰ But again he denied it. Then after a little while the bystanders again said to Peter, "Certainly you are one of them; for you are a Galilean." ⁷¹ But he began to curse, and he swore an oath, "I do not know this man you are talking about." ⁷² At that moment the cock crowed for the second time. Then Peter remembered that Jesus had said to him, "Before the cock crows twice, you will deny me three times." And he broke down and wept. (Mark 14:53-72)

While there are a few important differences (for example, Jesus' lack of speech), there are a few striking similarities, too. Here is a selection of the text from Acts (for a full account see Acts 6:8—7:60):

⁸ Stephen, full of grace and power, did great wonders and signs among the people. ⁹ Then some of those who belonged to the synagogue of the Freedmen (as it was called), Cyrenians, Alexandrians, and others of those from Cilicia and Asia, stood up and argued with Stephen. ¹⁰ But they could not withstand the wisdom and the Spirit with which he spoke. ¹¹ Then they secretly instigated some men to say, "We have heard him speak blasphemous words against Moses and God." ¹² They stirred up the people as well as the elders and the scribes; then they suddenly confronted him, seized him, and brought him before the council. ¹³ They set up false witnesses who said, "This man never stops saying things against this holy place and the law; ¹⁴ for we have heard

him say that this Jesus of Nazareth will destroy this place and will change the customs that Moses handed on to us." 15 And all who sat in the council looked intently at him, and they saw that his face was like the face of an angel.

7 1 Then the high priest asked him, "Are these things so?" 2 And Stephen replied: "Brothers and fathers, listen to me. The God of glory appeared to our ancestor Abraham when he was in Mesopotamia, before he lived in Haran, 3 and said to him, 'Leave your country and your relatives and go to the land that I will show you.' 4 Then he left the country of the Chaldeans and settled in Haran. After his father died, God had him move from there to this country in which you are now living. 5 He did not give him any of it as a heritage, not even a foot's length, but promised to give it to him as his possession and to his descendants after him, even though he had no child. 6 And God spoke in these terms, that his descendants would be resident aliens in a country belonging to others, who would enslave them and mistreat them during four hundred years. 7 'But I will judge the nation that they serve,' said God, 'and after that they shall come out and worship me in this place.' 8 Then he gave him the covenant of circumcision. And so Abraham became the father of Isaac and circumcised him on the eighth day; and Isaac became the father of Jacob, and Jacob of the twelve patriarchs.

51 "You stiff-necked people, uncircumcised in heart and ears, you are forever opposing the Holy Spirit, just as your ancestors used to do. 52 Which of the prophets did your ancestors not persecute? They killed those who foretold the coming of the Righteous One, and now you have become his betrayers and murderers. 53 You are the ones that received the law as ordained by angels, and yet you have not kept it."

54 When they heard these things, they became enraged and ground their teeth at Stephen. 55 But filled with the Holy Spirit, he gazed into heaven and saw the glory of God and Jesus standing at the right hand of God. 56 "Look," he said, "I see the heavens opened and the Son of Man standing at the right hand of God!" 57 But they covered their ears, and with a loud shout all rushed together against him. 58 Then they dragged him out of the city and began to stone him; and the witnesses laid their coats at the feet of a young man named Saul. 59 While they were stoning Stephen, he prayed, "Lord Jesus, receive my spirit." 60 Then he knelt down and cried out in a loud voice, "Lord, do not hold this sin against them." When he had said this, he died. (Acts 6:8—7:8, 51-60)

In both cases, these martyrs are shown to be vindicated at the expense of the "judge" who condemns them. In both cases, the martyr appeals to passages from Daniel 7 and Psalm 110. What are some other points of commonality?

Paul's Life

Most of the book of Acts tells of the missionary career of Paul. While we have several letters that convey Paul's mind and voice, we would know very little about his story without Acts. Paul does, however, speak of his own story in a couple of places. Consider these autobiographical "boasts":

¹⁶ I repeat, let no one think that I am a fool; but if you do, then accept me as a fool, so that I too may boast a little. ¹⁷ What I am saying in regard to this boastful confidence, I am saying not with the Lord's authority, but as a fool; ¹⁸ since many boast according to human standards, I will also boast. ¹⁹ For you gladly put up with fools, being wise yourselves! ²⁰ For you put up with it when someone makes slaves of you, or preys upon you, or takes advantage of you, or puts on airs, or gives you a slap in the face. ²¹ To my shame, I must say, we were too weak for that! But whatever anyone dares to boast of—I am speaking as a fool—I also dare to boast of that.

²² Are they Hebrews? So am I. Are they Israelites? So am I. Are they descendants of Abraham? So am I. ²³ Are they ministers of Christ? I am talking like a madman—I am a better one: with far greater labors, far more imprisonments, with countless floggings, and often near death. ²⁴ Five times I have received from the Jews the forty lashes minus one. ²⁵ Three times I was beaten with rods. Once I received a stoning. Three times I was shipwrecked; for a night and a day I was adrift at sea; ²⁶ on frequent journeys, in danger from rivers, danger from bandits, danger from my own people, danger from Gentiles, danger in the city, danger in the wilderness, danger at sea, danger from false brothers and sisters; ²⁷ in toil and hardship, through many a sleepless night, hungry and thirsty, often without food, cold and naked. ²⁸ And, besides other things, I am under daily pressure because of my anxiety for all the churches. ²⁹ Who is weak, and I am not

weak? Who is made to stumble, and I am not indignant? ³⁰ If I must boast, I will boast of the things that show my weakness. ³¹ The God and Father of the Lord Jesus (blessed be he forever!) knows that I do not lie. ³² In Damascus, the governor under King Aretas guarded the city of Damascus in order to seize me, ³³ but I was let down in a basket through a window in the wall, and escaped from his hands.

12 ¹ It is necessary to boast; nothing is to be gained by it, but I will go on to visions and revelations of the Lord. ² I know a person in Christ who fourteen years ago was caught up to the third heaven—whether in the body or out of the body I do not know; God knows. ³ And I know that such a person—whether in the body or out of the body I do not know; God knows— ⁴ was caught up into Paradise and heard things that are not to be told, that no mortal is permitted to repeat. ⁵ On behalf of such a one I will boast, but on my own behalf I will not boast, except of my weaknesses. ⁶ But if I wish to boast, I will not be a fool, for I will be speaking the truth. But I refrain from it, so that no one may think better of me than what is seen in me or heard from me, ⁷ even considering the exceptional character of the revelations. Therefore, to keep me from being too elated, a thorn was given me in the flesh, a messenger of Satan to torment me, to keep me from being too elated. ⁸ Three times I appealed to the Lord about this, that it would leave me, ⁹ but he said to me, "My grace is sufficient for you, for power is made perfect in weakness." So, I will boast all the more gladly of my

weaknesses, so that the power of Christ may dwell in me. [10] Therefore I am content with weaknesses, insults, hardships, persecutions, and calamities for the sake of Christ; for whenever I am weak, then I am strong. (2 Corinthians 11:16—12:10)

What sort of tone does Paul take here? Is this a passage that showcases Paul's strengths or weaknesses? Is it meant to be boastful or to convey humility?

The Character of Nero

As the apostles Peter, James, Paul and others continued to gain a following, new converts continued to negotiate an often hostile environment in the Roman Empire. Between the time of Peter's first Jerusalem community and the writing of Acts, the almost psychopathic Nero (37–68 C.E.) ruled the western world. Take a look at what Suetonius has to say about Nero (warning: this is description is quite repulsive):

XXVI. Petulancy, lewdness, luxury, avarice, and cruelty, he practised at first with reserve and in private, as if prompted to them only by the folly of youth; but, even then, the world was of opinion that they were the faults of his nature, and not of his age. After it was dark, he used to enter the taverns disguised in a cap or a wig, and ramble about the streets in sport, which was not void of mischief. He used to beat those he met coming home from supper; and, if they made any resistance, would wound them, and throw them into the common sewer. He broke open and robbed shops; establishing an auction at home for selling his booty. In the scuffles which took place on those occasions, he often ran the hazard of losing his eyes, and even his life;

being beaten almost to death by a senator, for handling his wife indecently. After this adventure, he never again ventured abroad at that time of night, without some tribunes following him at a little distance. In the day-time he would be carried to the theatre incognito in a litter, placing himself upon the upper part of the proscenium, where he not only witnessed the quarrels which arose on account of the performances, but also encouraged them. When they came to blows, and stones and pieces of broken benches began to fly about, he threw them plentifully amongst the people, and once even broke a praetor's head.

XXVII. His vices gaining strength by degrees, he laid aside his jocular amusements, and all disguise; breaking out into enormous crimes, without the least attempt to conceal them. His revels were prolonged from mid-day to midnight, while he was frequently refreshed by warm baths, and, in the summer time, by such as were cooled with snow. He often supped in public, in the Naumachia, with the sluices shut, or in the Campus Martius, or the Circus Maximus, being waited upon at table by common prostitutes of the town, and Syrian strumpets and glee-girls. As often as he went down the Tiber to Ostia, or coasted through the gulf of Baiae, booths furnished as brothels and eating-houses, were erected along the shore and river banks; before which stood matrons, who, like bawds and hostesses, allured him to land. It was also his custom to invite himself to supper with his friends; at one of which was expended no less than four millions of sesterces in chaplets, and at another something more in roses.

XXVIII. Besides the abuse of free-born lads, and the debauch of married women, he committed a rape upon Rubria, a Vestal Virgin. He was upon the point of marrying Acte, his freedwoman, having suborned some men of consular rank to swear that she was of royal descent. He gelded the boy Sporus, and endeavoured to transform him into a woman. He even went so far as to marry him, with all the usual formalities of a marriage settlement, the rose-coloured nuptial veil, and a numerous company at the wedding. When the ceremony was over, he had him conducted like a bride to his own house, and treated him as his wife. It was jocularly observed by some person, "that it would have been well for mankind, had such a wife fallen to the lot of his father Domitius." This Sporus he carried about with him in a litter round the solemn assemblies and fairs of Greece, and afterwards at Rome through the Sigillaria, dressed in the rich attire of an empress; kissing him from time to time as they rode together. That he entertained an incestuous passion for his mother, but was deterred by her enemies, for fear that this haughty and overbearing woman should, by her compliance, get him entirely into her power, and govern in every thing, was universally believed; especially after he had introduced amongst his concubines a strumpet, who was reported to have a strong resemblance to Agrippina.

XXIX. He prostituted his own chastity to such a degree, that after he had defiled every part of his person with some unnatural pollution, he at last invented an extraordinary kind of diversion; which was, to be let out of a den in the arena, covered with the skin of a wild beast, and then assail with violence the private parts both of men and women, while they were bound to stakes. After he had vented his furious passion upon them, he finished the play in the embraces of his freedman Doryphorus, to whom he was married in the same way that Sporus had been married to himself; imitating the cries and shrieks of young virgins, when they are ravished. I have been informed from numerous sources, that he firmly believed, no man in the world to be chaste, or any part of his person undefiled; but that most men concealed that vice, and were cunning enough to keep it secret. To those, therefore, who frankly owned their unnatural lewdness, he forgave all other crimes.

Source: Suetonius, "Nero Claudius Caesar" in *The Lives of the Caesars*, trans. Alexander Thomson, M.D.; http://www.gutenberg.org/files/6400/6400-h/6400-h.htm

Questions for Group Discussion

1. How does the giving of the Holy Spirit relate to the hope for social renewal?
2. What is the purpose of the story of Stephen's execution?
3. What do we learn about Paul's character? What motivates him?

Questions for Reflection

1. Why is the story of early Christianity such a violent history?

2. To what extent does Acts idealize Christian leaders and villianize other kinds of leaders?

14

The Pauline Letters: Apostolic Advice
to Early Churches

Summary and Learning Objectives

1. Paul's undisputed letters occupy a central place in the history of emerging Christianity and New Testament theology. Not only to they give us glimpses of the problems faced by various churches within Paul's sphere of influence, they give us the best data for reconstructing Paul's thought world. After reading this chapter (alongside chapter 14 of Sumney's text), the reader should be able *to speak to Paul's inclusivism when it comes to socio-economic boundaries.*

2. After reading this chapter (alongside chapter 14 of Sumney's text), the reader should be able *to speak to Paul's exclusivism when it comes to boundaries of worship.*

3. After reading this chapter (alongside chapter 14 of Sumney's text), the reader should be able *to identify a few key themes in Paul's letters.*

4. After reading this chapter (alongside chapter 14 of Sumney's text), the reader should be able *to explain why the commemorative act of communion was important to Paul.*

Key Terms

Communion   A term used for the Lord's Supper that emphasizes that the participants are sharing the meal with one another, Christ, and God.

Letter   Written form of communication intended to address the specific people named and usually to engage them personally and specifically.

Literary epistle   A formal letter intended to be read by a public audience.

Passover   The festival within Judaism that commemorates the exodus from Egypt. It is a pilgrimage feast that also celebrates the New Year. It is during the time of this festival that Jesus is crucified.

Paul   A persecutor of the church who has an experience of the risen Christ on the way to Damascus that leads him to become a believer. He becomes the apostle and leading missionary to the gentiles in the first generation of the church. His letters to his churches account for more books in the New Testament than any other author.

Philemon   Owner of Onesimus and primary addressee of one of Paul's letters.

Key Themes

▸ Church unity was of the utmost importance to Paul

▸ Paul draws upon well-known Christian tradition, but also draws heavily from the cultural categories of first-century Judaism

▸ Much like Luke, Paul's vision for the church hinges on socio-economic equality

Primary Text

Philemon and Onesimus

Central to Paul's message is a collapse of socio-economic barriers. In order to get a good view of how Paul's words resulted in real world action, read the letter to Philemon (the entire letter is only 25 verses long). Paul is probably sending this letter with a slave, or former slave, named Onesimus. The letter is addressed to his (former?) slave owner, named Philemon.

> [1] Paul, a prisoner of Christ Jesus, and Timothy our brother,
>
> To Philemon our dear friend and co-worker, [2] to Apphia our sister, to Archippus our fellow soldier, and to the church in your house:
>
> [3] Grace to you and peace from God our Father and the Lord Jesus Christ.
>
> [4] When I remember you in my prayers, I always thank my God [5] because I hear of your love for all the saints and your faith toward the Lord Jesus. [6] I pray that the sharing of your faith may become effective when you perceive all the good that we may do for Christ. [7] I have indeed received much joy and encouragement from your love, because the hearts of the saints have been refreshed through you, my brother.
>
> [8] For this reason, though I am bold enough in Christ to command you to do your duty, [9] yet I would rather appeal to you on the basis of love—and I, Paul, do this as an old man, and now also as a prisoner of Christ Jesus. [10] I am appealing to you for my child, Onesimus, whose father I have become during my imprisonment. [11] Formerly he was useless to you, but now he is indeed useful both to you and to me. [12] I am sending him, that is, my own heart, back to you. [13] I wanted to keep him with me, so that he might be of service to me in your place during my imprisonment for the gospel; [14] but I preferred to do nothing without your consent, in order that your good deed might be voluntary and not something forced. [15] Perhaps this is the reason he was separated from you for a while, so that you might have him back forever, [16] no longer as a slave but more than a slave, a beloved brother—especially to me but how much more to you, both in the flesh and in the Lord.

[17] So if you consider me your partner, welcome him as you would welcome me. [18] If he has wronged you in any way, or owes you anything, charge that to my account. [19] I, Paul, am writing this with my own hand: I will repay it. I say nothing about your owing me even your own self. [20] Yes, brother, let me have this benefit from you in the Lord! Refresh my heart in Christ. [21] Confident of your obedience, I am writing to you, knowing that you will do even more than I say.

[22] One thing more—prepare a guest room for me, for I am hoping through your prayers to be restored to you.

[23] Epaphras, my fellow prisoner in Christ Jesus, sends greetings to you, [24] and so do Mark, Aristarchus, Demas, and Luke, my fellow workers.

[25] The grace of the Lord Jesus Christ be with your spirit. (Philemon 1-25)

Notice the tone Paul takes at the beginning and end of his letter to Philemon. Notice also the passive-aggressive demand for social equality. What does this letter suggest of Paul's overall view of Christian unity?

Making Good with Creation

Paul seems to believe that the salvation of humanity will in some way include the salvation of all creation. Consider Romans 8:18-27:

[18] I consider that the sufferings of this present time are not worth comparing with the glory about to be revealed to us. [19] For the creation waits with eager longing for the revealing of the children of God; [20] for the creation was subjected to futility, not of its own will but by the will of the one who subjected it, in hope [21] that the creation itself will be set free from its bondage to decay and will obtain the freedom of the glory of the children of God. [22] We know that the whole creation has been groaning in labor pains until now; [23] and not only the creation, but we ourselves, who have the first fruits of the Spirit, groan inwardly while we wait for adoption, the redemption of our bodies. [24] For in hope we were saved. Now hope that is seen is not hope. For who hopes for what is seen? [25] But if we hope for what we do not see, we wait for it with patience.

[26] Likewise the Spirit helps us in our weakness; for we do not know how to pray as we ought, but that very Spirit intercedes with sighs too deep for words. [27] And God, who searches the heart, knows what is the mind of the Spirit, because the Spirit intercedes for the saints according to the will of God.

Here Paul emphasizes the "vertical" relationship between humanity and Creator, but connects this to the "horizontal" relationship between humanity and creation. In this context, Paul's claims that "the creation was subjected to futility, not of its own will but by the will of the one who subjected it" (v. 20). Take a look at Genesis 3:17 and answer this question: *who is the "one" who subjected the earth to futility?*

Communion

Paul very rarely quotes Jesus. It is important to remember that the biblical Gospels are not known to Paul. It does seem, however, that Paul has learned and remembers Jesus' last Passover meal with his disciples. It seems that this traditional meal has taken on a new significance in Christian memory. Compare the account in Luke's Gospel to Paul's memory and interpretation of this meal (1 Corinthians 11:17-34). Keep in mind that Paul is probably writing several decades or more before Luke:

> [17] Now in the following instructions I do not commend you, because when you come together it is not for the better but for the worse. [18] For, to begin with, when you come together as a church, I hear that there are divisions among you; and to some extent I believe it. [19] Indeed, there have to be factions among you, for only so will it become clear who among you are genuine. [20] When you come together, it is not really to eat the Lord's supper. [21] For when the time comes to eat, each of you goes ahead with your own supper, and one goes hungry and another becomes drunk. [22] What! Do you not have homes to eat and drink in? Or do you show contempt for the church of God and humiliate those who have nothing? What should I say to you? Should I commend you? In this matter I do not commend you!
>
> [23] For I received from the Lord what I also handed on to you, that the Lord Jesus on the night when he was betrayed took a loaf of bread, [24] and when he had given thanks, he broke it and said, "This is my body that is for you. Do this in remembrance of me." [25] In the same way he took the cup also, after supper, saying, "This cup is the new covenant in my blood. Do this, as often as you drink it, in remembrance of me." [26] For as often as you eat this bread and drink the cup, you proclaim the Lord's death until he comes. [27] Whoever,

therefore, eats the bread or drinks the cup of the Lord in an unworthy manner will be answerable for the body and blood of the Lord. [28] Examine yourselves, and only then eat of the bread and drink of the cup. [29] For all who eat and drink without discerning the body, eat and drink judgment against themselves. [30] For this reason many of you are weak and ill, and some have died. [31] But if we judged ourselves, we would not be judged. [32] But when we are judged by the Lord, we are disciplined so that we may not be condemned along with the world. [33] So then, my brothers and sisters, when you come together to eat, wait for one another. [34] If you are hungry, eat at home, so that when you come together, it will not be for your condemnation. About the other things I will give instructions when I come. (1 Corinthians 11:17-34)

Luke's account reads:

> [13] So they went and found everything as he had told them; and they prepared the Passover meal. [14] When the hour came, he took his place at the table, and the apostles with him. [15] He said to them, "I have eagerly desired to eat this Passover with you before I suffer; [16] for I tell you, I will not eat it until it is fulfilled in the kingdom of God." [17] Then he took a cup, and after giving thanks he said, "Take this and divide it among yourselves; [18] for I tell you that from now on I will not drink of the fruit of the vine until the kingdom of God comes." [19] Then he took a loaf of bread, and when he had given thanks, he broke it and gave it to them, saying, "This is my body, which is given for

you. Do this in remembrance of me." [20] And he did the same with the cup after supper, saying, "This cup that is poured out for you is the new covenant in my blood.

[21] But see, the one who betrays me is with me, and his hand is on the table. [22] For the Son of Man is going as it has been determined, but woe to that one by whom he is betrayed!" [23] Then they began to ask one another, which one of them it could be who would do this. (Luke 22:13-23)

This is a great example of how a common Christian memory can be used in two ways for two different purposes. Why is Paul interested in the commemorative practice of the "last supper"? Why is Luke interested in the commemorative practice of the "passover"?

The Wisdom of God

While the heart of Paul's message is the inclusion of outsiders, he sees an important distinction between insiders and outsiders. Among the differences, according to Paul, is the outsider's inability to comprehence God's wisdom. 1 Corinthians 2:6-16 reads:

[6] Yet among the mature we do speak wisdom, though it is not a wisdom of this age or of the rulers of this age, who are doomed to perish. [7] But we speak God's wisdom, secret and hidden, which God decreed before the ages for our glory. [8] None of the rulers of this age understood this; for if they had, they would not have crucified the Lord of glory. [9] But, as it is written,

"What no eye has seen, nor ear heard,
    nor the human heart conceived,
what God has prepared for those who love
    him"—

[10] these things God has revealed to us through the Spirit; for the Spirit searches everything, even the depths of God. [11] For what human being knows what is truly human except the human spirit that is within? So also no one comprehends what is truly God's except the Spirit of God. [12] Now we have received not the spirit of the world, but the Spirit that is from God, so that we may understand the gifts bestowed on us by God. [13] And we speak of these things in words not taught by human wisdom but taught by the Spirit, interpreting spiritual things to those who are spiritual.

[14] Those who are unspiritual do not receive the gifts of God's Spirit, for they are foolishness to them, and they are unable to understand them because they are spiritually discerned. [15] Those who are spiritual discern all things, and they are themselves subject to no one else's scrutiny.

[16] "For who has known the mind of the Lord
    so as to instruct him?"

But we have the mind of Christ.

In this passage Paul demonstrates his belief that the gathering of believers is a holy and spiritual people, enlightened in a way that people outside are not.

The Book of Wisdom, a Jewish text that was written more than a century before Paul's life, the purported voiced of Solomon reflects on the inability of mortals to comprehend divine Wisdom. Wisdom 9:9-18 (NRSV) reads:

[9] With you is wisdom, she who knows your works and was present when you made the world; she understands what is pleasing in your sight and what is right according

to your commandments. [10] Send her forth from the holy heavens, and from the throne of your glory send her, that she may labor at my side, and that I may learn what is pleasing to you. [11] For she knows and understands all things, and she will guide me wisely in my actions and guard me with her glory. [12] Then my works will be acceptable, and I shall judge your people justly, and shall be worthy of the throne of my father. [13] For who can learn the counsel of God? Or who can discern what the Lord wills? [14] For the reasoning of mortals is worthless, and our designs are likely to fail; [15] for a perishable body weighs down the soul, and this earthy tent burdens the thoughtful mind. [16] We can hardly guess at what is on earth, and what is at hand we find with labor; but who has traced out what is in the heavens? [17] Who has learned your counsel, unless you have given wisdom and sent your holy spirit from on high? [18] And thus the paths of those on earth were set right, and people were taught what pleases you, and were saved by wisdom."

Notice that in this passage, the "holy spirit" mediates Wisdom to certain people on Earth. What other similarities are there between this passage and Paul's thought?

Circumcision

Church members were not the only ones arguing about whether circumcision was necessary for a person to be included among the people of God. Josephus tells the story of king Izates of Adiabene (an area north and east of Palestine), who decides to worship only God and is ready to be circumcised to become a part of God's people. But his Jewish teacher Ananias tells him not to be circumcised, assuring him that "he might worship God without being circumcised, even though he did resolve to follow the Jewish law entirely, which worship of God was of a superior nature to circumcision" (*Ant.* 20.41). But when another teacher named Eleazar arrived and was asked about this matter, he replied:

> "Thou dost not consider, O king! that thou unjustly breakest the principal of those laws, and art injurious to God himself, [by omitting to be circumcised]; for thou oughtest not only to read them, but chiefly to practice what they enjoin thee. How long wilt thou continue uncircumcised? But if thou hast not yet read the law about circumcision, and dost not know how great impiety thou art guilty of by neglecting it, read it now." When the king had heard what he said, he delayed the thing no longer, but retired to another room, and sent for a surgeon, and did what he was commanded to do." (*Ant* 20.44-46)

Source: William Whiston, trans., *The Works of Flavius Josephus* (Worcester: Isaiah Thomas, 1793)

This episode suggests that various kinds of Jews were drawing different conclusions about whether gentiles needed to accept circumcision to be faithful worshippers of God. How does this influence the way you hear the debate as it surfaces in Paul's letters?

Questions for Group Discussion

1. What does communion symbolize for Paul?
2. What did circumcision symbolize for most first-century Jews?
3. What is the relationship between humanity and the earth according to Paul?

Questions for Reflection

1. Why is Paul so committed to socio-economic equality but so willing to exclude people of differing beliefs?

2. What does Paul's letter to Philemon suggest about the ethics of institutional slavery?

15

The Disputed Pauline Letters: Continuing Advice in Paul's Name

Summary and Learning Objectives

1. The Deutero-Paulines, in many ways, extend the voice and ideas of Paul and expand them to include a wider range of ideas and voices within late first-century Christianity. These letters give us glimpses of how Christianity continued to evolve beyond Paul's sphere of influence. After reading this chapter (alongside chapter 15 of Sumney's text), the reader should be able *to indentify a few features of prison life in the first century.*
2. After reading this chapter (alongside chapter 15 of Sumney's text), the reader should be able *to speak to a few different first-century Jewish ideas concerning God's foreknowledge.*
3. After reading this chapter (alongside chapter 15 of Sumney's text), the reader should be able *to better explain how the metaphor of a community "temple" was used by early Christians.*

Key Terms

Body of Christ   A metaphor for the church that indicates the close relationship among members (because they are members of the same body) and that the church is the presence of Christ in the world. In early usage, it was applied only to individual congregations. As time passed, the image enlarged so that the church worldwide was identified as the one cosmic body of Christ.

Deutero-Paulines   The writings in the New Testament that claim to be written by Paul, but that most scholars believe were written by someone else after his death. Those most likely to fall into this category are Ephesians, 1 and 2 Timothy, and Titus. Many scholars also think that Colossians and 2 Thessalonians were written after Paul died. These writings were intended to apply Paul's teaching to a new situation.

Man of Lawlessness A person mentioned in 2 Thessalonians as evidence that the "Day of the Lord" had not yet occurred. Although he has been identified in many ways, we cannot be certain of his identity except to say that he was someone who lived in the late first century, otherwise the original readers of 2 Thessalonians would not have known who he is, which was necessary for the letter's argument.

Second coming Time when Christ returns to earth, bringing God's judgment, the resurrection of the dead, and the end of the world as it is now known.

Key Themes

▶ The early Christians continue to struggle with unity and Paul's voice is utilized again to exhort them toward togetherness

▶ The metaphor of a "temple" community continues to be employed to promote unity in wealth, social standing, and worship

▶ Early Christianity has several points of similarity with the Jewish worshiping community at the Dead Sea

Primary Text

Prison Life

Diodorus Sculus (first century B.C.E.) wrote a description of the prison life of King Perseus. After his defeat by the Romans, Perseus seems to have been given a prison cell with commoners. This may well provide us with an analogy of episodes the apostle Paul's life in jail. We should, however, keep in mind the possibility that Paul experience was much worse than this description:

Perseus, the last king of Macedonia, whose relations with the Romans were often amicable, but who also repeatedly fought against them with a not inconsiderable army, was finally defeated and taken captive by Aemilius, who for this victory celebrated a magnificent triumph. The misfortunes that Perseus encountered were so great that his sufferings seem like the inventions of fiction, yet even so he was not willing to be quit of life. For before the senate had decided on the penalty he should suffer, one of the urban praetors had him cast with his children into the prison at Alba. This prison is a deep underground dungeon, no larger than a nine-couch room, dark, and noisome from the large numbers committed to the place, who were men under condemnation on capital charges, for most of this category were incarcerated there at that period. With so many shut up in such close quarters, the poor wretches were reduced to the physical appearance of brutes, and since their food and everything pertaining to their other needs was all foully commingled, a stench so terrible assailed anyone who drew near that it could scarcely be endured. There for seven days Perseus remained, in such sorry plight that he begged succour even from men of the meanest stamp, whose food was the prison ration. They, indeed, affected by the magnitude of his misfortune, in which they shared, wept and generously gave him a portion of whatever they received. A sword with which to kill himself was thrown down to him, and a noose for hanging, with full freedom to use them as he might wish.

Nothing, however, seems so sweet to those who have suffered misfortune as life itself, even when their sufferings would warrant death. And at last he would have died under these deprivations had not Marcus Aemilius, leader of the senate, to maintain both his own principles and his country's code of equity, indignantly admonished the senate, even if they had nothing to fear from men, at least to respect the Nemesis that dogs those who arrogantly abuse their power. As a result, Perseus was placed in more suitable custody, and, because of the senate's kindness, sustained himself by vain hopes, only to meet at last an end that matched his earlier misfortunes. For after clinging to life for two years, he offended the barbarians who were his guards, and was prevented from sleeping until he died of it.

Source: *Diodorus Siculus*, Library of History, Vol. 11; Loeb Classical Library 409, trans. F. R. Walton; (Cambridge: Harvard University Press, 1957), 335–37.

God's Foreknowledge

The author of Ephesians begins the letter by claiming that those who are blessed "in Christ" were selected by God "before the foundation of the world." Ephesians 1:3-10 reads:

> [3] Blessed be the God and Father of our Lord Jesus Christ, who has blessed us in Christ with every spiritual blessing in the heavenly places, [4] just as he chose us in Christ before the foundation of the world to be holy and blameless before him in love. [5] He destined us for adoption as his children through Jesus Christ, according to the good pleasure of his will, [6] to the praise of his glorious grace that he freely bestowed on us in the Beloved. [7] In him we have redemption through his blood, the forgiveness of our trespasses, according to the riches of his grace [8] that he lavished on us. With all wisdom and insight [9] he has made known to us the mystery of his will, according to his good pleasure that he set forth in Christ, [10] as a plan for the fullness of time, to gather up all things in him, things in heaven and things on earth.

The idea that God predetermines those who will receive blessing and cursing seems to have a parallel in the Dead Sea Scrolls (CD 2:4b-13):

> He is very patient and forgiving, covering the sin of those who repent of wrongdoing. But Strength, Might, and great Wrath in the flames of fire with all the angels of destruction shall come against all who rebel against the proper way and who despise the law, until they are without remnant of survivor, for God had not chosen them from ancient eternity. Before they were created, He knew what they would do. So He rejected the generations of old and turned away from the land until they were gone.
>
> He knows the times of appearance and the number and exact times of everything that has ever existed and ever will exist before it happens in the proper time, for all eternity. And in all of these times, He has arranged that there should be for Himself people called by name, so that there would always be survivors on the earth, replenishing the surface of the earth with

their descendants. He taught them through those anointed by the holy spirit, the seers of truth. He explicitly called them by name. But whoever He had rejected He caused to stray.

Source: M. Wise, M. Abegg, and E. Cook, eds., *The Dead Sea Scrolls: A New Translation* (San Francisco: HarperSanFrancisco, 1996), 52–53.

Notice in the this passage that the author of this text expects certain figures to rise up and oppose the "proper way" and the "seers of truth." Even so, there is a firm expectation that these figures are predestined for failure. With this in mind, consider the author of 2 Thessalonians's expectation for a figure he calls "the lawless one" (also translated as "the Man of Lawlessness") to emerge before Christ's final victory at his "second coming":

> [1] As to the coming of our Lord Jesus Christ and our being gathered together to him, we beg you, brothers and sisters, [2] not to be quickly shaken in mind or alarmed, either by spirit or by word or by letter, as though from us, to the effect that the day of the Lord is already here.
>
> [3] Let no one deceive you in any way; for that day will not come unless the rebellion comes first and the lawless one is revealed, the one destined for destruction. [4] He opposes and exalts himself above every so-called god or object of worship, so that he takes his seat in the temple of God, declaring himself to be God. [5] Do you not remember that I told you these things when I was still with you? [6] And you know what is now restraining him, so that he may be revealed when his time comes. [7] For the mystery of lawlessness is already at work, but only until the one who now restrains it is removed. [8] And then the lawless one will be revealed, whom the Lord Jesus will destroy with the breath of his mouth, annihilating him by the manifestation of his coming. [9] The coming of the lawless one is apparent in the working of Satan, who uses all power, signs, lying wonders, [10] and every kind of wicked deception for those who are perishing, because they refused to love the truth and so be saved. [11] For this reason God sends them a powerful delusion, leading them to believe what is false, [12] so that all who have not believed the truth but took pleasure in unrighteousness will be condemned. (2 Thessalonians 2:1-12)

In both of these visions for the future, the good figures and bad figures are set apart by their relationship with the truth. In other words, those who represent the people of God are revealed by their truthfulness, whereas those who oppose God are deceitful. What are some other points of contact between these texts?

A Temple Community

Paul tells the community at Corinth that they are supposed to function as the ideal temple. They are to demonstrate unity and equality in worship, economics, and social standing. Paul writes: ". . . do you not know that you are God's temple and that God's Spirit dwells in you? If anyone destroys God's temple, God will destroy that person. For God's temple is holy, and you are that temple" (1 Corinthians 3:16-17). It is important to keep in mind that the "body of Christ" is a collective identity. It refers to the entire worshiping (corporate) body. So Paul is mixing metaphors in this case. The idea that the early

Christians were a metaphorical temple can be seen also in Ephesians 2:13-22:

> [13] But now in Christ Jesus you who once were far off have been brought near by the blood of Christ.
>
> [14] For he is our peace; in his flesh he has made both groups into one and has broken down the dividing wall, that is, the hostility between us. [15] He has abolished the law with its commandments and ordinances, that he might create in himself one new humanity in place of the two, thus making peace, [16] and might reconcile both groups to God in one body through the cross, thus putting to death that hostility through it. [17] So he came and proclaimed peace to you who were far off and peace to those who were near; [18] for through him both of us have access in one Spirit to the Father. [19] So then you are no longer strangers and aliens, but you are citizens with the saints and also members of the household of God, [20] built upon the foundation of the apostles and prophets, with Christ Jesus himself as the cornerstone. [21] In him the whole structure is joined together and grows into a holy temple in the Lord; [22] in whom you also are built together spiritually into a dwelling place for God.

Notice the architectural metaphor, drawing from Psalm 118:22: "The stone that the builders rejected has become the chief cornerstone." This passage extends the architectural metaphor by referring to Christ and the apostles as the foundation of the structure. Given the use of this temple metaphor, consider the similar self-understanding by the Dead Sea community. They call themselves the "Yahad" and believed themselves to function as a temple ("Holy of Holies").

> When, united by all these precepts, such men as these come to be a community in Israel, they shall establish eternal truth guided by the instruction of His holy spirit. They shall atone for the guilt of transgression and the rebellion of sin, becoming an acceptable sacrifice for the land through the flesh of burnt offerings. the fat of sacrificial portions, and prayer, becoming— as it were—justice itself, a sweet savor of righteousness and blameless behavior, a pleasing freewill offering. At that time the men of the Yahad shall withdraw, the holy house of Aaron uniting as a Holy of Holies, and the synagogue of Israel as those who walk blamelessly. The sons of Aaron alone shall have authority in judicial and financial matters. They shall decide on governing precepts tor the men of the Yahad and on money matters for the holy men who walk blamelessly. Their wealth is not to be admired with that of rebellious men, who have failed to cleanse their path by separating from perversity and walking blamelessly. They shall deviate from none of the teachings of the Law, whereby they would walk in their willful heart completely. They shall govern themselves using the original precepts by which the men of the Yahad began to be instructed, doing so until there come the Prophet and the Messiahs of Aaron and Israel. (1QS IX.3-11)

Source: M. Wise, M. Abegg, and E. Cook, eds., *The Dead Sea Scrolls: A New Translation* (San Francisco: HarperSanFrancisco, 1996), 139.

Notice here that the author of this text believes that the community members function as a metaphorical sacrifice. It is unclear whether they themselves are the metaphorical sacrifice or if their prayers function as such. In either case, they believe themselves to be the true priesthood (as opposed to the Jerusalem temple establishment). A striking difference between this group and emerging Christianity is that the Dead Sea community expresses hope for multiple messiahs.

Questions for Group Discussion

1. What would it mean for a group to practice social, economic, and worshiping equality? Is such a practice altogether impossible in an individualistic culture?
2. Many of the authors of the New Testament believed that there would be particular signs revealed to mark the "second coming" of Christ. Can you name at least one such sign in 2 Thessalonians 2:1-12? What are some others beyond this passage?

Questions for Reflection

1. What does it say about early Christianity that many of its sacred texts were penned in a prison cell? How has this shaped Christian identity?

2. Do you think that early readers of Paul might have had more in common with Roman citizens or Dead Sea community members? To what extent might both be true?

16

Hebrews and the General Epistles: Messages for Broader Audiences

Summary and Learning Objectives

1. The General Letters and Hebrews occupies an enigmatic space in Christian tradition. Some elements of these texts have become central to Christian doctrine. Other elements of these texts have puzzled readers for centuries. After reading this chapter (alongside chapter 16 of Sumney's text), the reader should be able *to explain the significance of Jesus' title as "High Priest."*
2. After reading this chapter (alongside chapter 16 of Sumney's text), the reader should be able *to identify elements of supersessionism in Hebrews.*
3. After reading this chapter (alongside chapter 16 of Sumney's text), the reader should be able *to offer a summary of the Myth of the Watchers.*

Key Terms

Christology The study of the nature and work of Christ. This field of study considers what it means to talk about Jesus Christ as human or divine (or both) and defines what the ministry and death of Christ accomplished.

The Myth of the Watchers A legend that was popular before and during the writing of the New Testament among Jews and Christians. This legend was a historical fiction based on the story of Noah's flood. According to the legend, the flood was sent to wipe out divine-human hybrids (or giants). The souls of these monsters live on after death as disembodied demons.

Supersessionism The belief that the church took the place of Israel as God's people. Even though this view has often been attributed to Paul, he was not a supersessionist. He believed that Israel remains in a special covenant relationship with God.

High Priest An office in the Jerusalem temple. This descendant of Aaron entered the Holy of Holies to make atonement for his house and for the people on the Day of Atonement. He offered sacrifices for the sins of the priests and people.

Key Themes

▸ In exalting Christ, some Christians denigrated non-Christian Jewish worship

▸ The metaphor of the Church as "temple" evolved into a belief in Jesus as "High Priest"

▸ Popular Jewish legends influenced some of the writers of the New Testament

Primary Text

Supersessionism

A key emphasis of Hebrews is the argument that the blessings bestowed on those who are in Christ are superior to those of the Mosaic covenant. This can be understood as one form of "supersessionism." The author believes that the worship experience as mediated by Christ outmodes the worship experience of Israel as mediated by the Jerusalem temple. While this belief has been central to traditional Christian doctrine, it must be acknowledged that supersessionism has had tragic and horrific consequences for Jewish-Christian relations through the centuries. Christian violence against Jews have often been justified or motivated by texts like the following:

> [12] Take care, brothers and sisters, that none of you may have an evil, unbelieving heart that turns away from the living God. [13] But exhort one another every day, as long as it is called "today," so that none of you may be hardened by the deceitfulness of sin. [14] For we have become partners of Christ, if only we hold our first confidence firm to

the end. [15] As it is said, "Today, if you hear his voice, do not harden your hearts as in the rebellion." [16] Now who were they who heard and yet were rebellious? Was it not all those who left Egypt under the leadership of Moses? [17] But with whom was he angry forty years? Was it not those who sinned, whose bodies fell in the wilderness? [18] And to whom did he swear that they would not enter his rest, if not to those who were disobedient? [19] So we see that they were unable to enter because of unbelief.

4 [1] Therefore, while the promise of entering his rest is still open, let us take care that none of you should seem to have failed to reach it. [2] For indeed the good news came to us just as to them; but the message they heard did not benefit them, because they were not united by faith with those who listened. [3] For we who have believed enter that rest, just as God has said, "As in my anger I swore, 'They shall not enter my rest,'" though his works were finished at the foundation of the world. [4] For in one place it speaks about the seventh day as follows, "And God rested on the seventh day from all his works." [5] And again in this place it says, "They shall not enter my rest." [6] Since therefore it remains open for some to enter it, and those who formerly received the good news failed to enter because of disobedience, [7] again he sets a certain day— "today"—saying through David much later, in the words already quoted, "Today, if you hear his voice, do not harden your hearts." [8] For if Joshua had given them rest, God would not speak later about another day. [9] So then, a sabbath rest still remains for the

people of God; [10] for those who enter God's rest also cease from their labors as God did from his.

[11] Let us therefore make every effort to enter that rest, so that no one may fall through such disobedience as theirs. [12] Indeed, the word of God is living and active, sharper than any two-edged sword, piercing until it divides soul from spirit, joints from marrow; it is able to judge the thoughts and intentions of the heart. [13] And before him no creature is hidden, but all are naked and laid bare to the eyes of the one to whom we must render an account. [14] Since, then, we have a great high priest who has passed through the heavens, Jesus, the Son of God, let us hold fast to our confession. [15] For we do not have a high priest who is unable to sympathize with our weaknesses, but we have one who in every respect has been tested as we are, yet without sin. [16] Let us therefore approach the throne of grace with boldness, so that we may receive mercy and find grace to help in time of need.

5 [1] Every high priest chosen from among mortals is put in charge of things pertaining to God on their behalf, to offer gifts and sacrifices for sins. [2] He is able to deal gently with the ignorant and wayward, since he himself is subject to weakness; [3] and because of this he must offer sacrifice for his own sins as well as for those of the people. [4] And one does not presume to take this honor, but takes it only when called by God, just as Aaron was. [5] So also Christ did not glorify himself in becoming a high priest, but was appointed by the one who said to him, "You are my Son, today I have begotten you"; [6] as he says also in another place, "You are a priest forever, according to the order of Melchizedek." [7] In the days of his flesh, Jesus offered up prayers and supplications, with loud cries and tears, to the one who was able to save him from death, and he was heard because of his reverent submission. [8] Although he was a Son, he learned obedience through what he suffered; [9] and having been made perfect, he became the source of eternal salvation for all who obey him, [10] having been designated by God a high priest according to the order of Melchizedek. (Hebrews 3:12—5:10)

Given that many previous Christians (including writers of the New Testament) described the body of Christ as a "temple," it is not surprising to see the author of this letter refer to Christ as the "high priest." The author, however, takes this line of thought a step further by suggesting that the Jerusalem Temple has been outmoded:

[1] Now even the first covenant had regulations for worship and an earthly sanctuary. [2] For a tent was constructed, the first one, in which were the lampstand, the table, and the bread of the Presence; this is called the Holy Place. [3] Behind the second curtain was a tent called the Holy of Holies. [4] In it stood the golden altar of incense and the ark of the covenant overlaid on all sides with gold, in which there were a golden urn holding the manna, and Aaron's rod that budded, and the tablets of the covenant; [5] above it were the cherubim of glory overshadowing the mercy seat. Of these things we cannot speak now in detail. [6] Such preparations

having been made, the priests go continually into the first tent to carry out their ritual duties; [7] but only the high priest goes into the second, and he but once a year, and not without taking the blood that he offers for himself and for the sins committed unintentionally by the people.

[8] By this the Holy Spirit indicates that the way into the sanctuary has not yet been disclosed as long as the first tent is still standing. [9] This is a symbol of the present time, during which gifts and sacrifices are offered that cannot perfect the conscience of the worshiper, [10] but deal only with food and drink and various baptisms, regulations for the body imposed until the time comes to set things right. [11] But when Christ came as a high priest of the good things that have come, then through the greater and perfect tent (not made with hands, that is, not of this creation), [12] he entered once for all into the Holy Place, not with the blood of goats and calves, but with his own blood, thus obtaining eternal redemption. [13] For if the blood of goats and bulls, with the sprinkling of the ashes of a heifer, sanctifies those who have been defiled so that their flesh is purified, [14] how much more will the blood of Christ, who through the eternal Spirit offered himself without blemish to God, purify our conscience from dead works to worship the living God! (Hebrews 9:1-14)

Is the author of this letter is arguing that Jewish worship apart from Christ is obsolete? Given the emphasis on the temple, do you think this document was written before or after the destruction of the Jerusalem temple in 70 C.E.?

1 Clement

Many early Christian texts, including letters by early Christian leaders, did not make it into the New Testament. One such letter is 1 Clement (there is also a 2 Clement). The traditional view is that the letter was written by Clement of Rome (an important Church leader in the first century), although this is far from certain. This text contains many features that are common to New Testament letters, including a high view of Christ as Lord (a high "Christology"). Much like Hebrews this author refers to Jesus as the "High Priest." Included below are chapters 36 and 38:

> 36 This is the way, beloved, in which we find our Saviour, even Jesus Christ, the High Priest of all our offerings, the defender and helper of our infirmity. By Him we look up to the heights of heaven. By Him we behold, as in a glass, His immaculate and most excellent visage. By Him are the eyes of our hearts opened. By Him our foolish and darkened understanding blossoms up anew towards His marvellous light. By Him the Lord has willed that we should taste of immortal knowledge, "who, being the brightness of His majesty, is by so much greater than the angels, as He has by inheritance obtained a more excellent name than they." For it is thus written, "Who makes His angels spirits, and His ministers a flame of fire." But concerning His Son the Lord spoke thus: "You are my Son, today have I begotten You. Ask of Me, and I will give You the heathen for Your inheritance, and the uttermost parts of the earth for Your possession." And again He says to Him, "Sit at My right hand, until I make Your enemies Your footstool." But who are His

enemies? All the wicked, and those who set themselves to oppose the will of God.

38 Let our whole body, then, be preserved in, Christ Jesus; and let every one be subject to his neighbour, according to the special gift bestowed upon him. Let the strong not despise the weak, and let the weak show respect to the strong. Let the rich man provide for the wants of the poor; and let the poor man bless God, because He has given him one by whom his need may be supplied. Let the wise man display his wisdom, not by [mere] words, but through good deeds. Let the humble not bear testimony to himself, but leave witness to be borne to him by another. Let him that is pure in the flesh not grow proud of it, and boast, knowing that it was another who bestowed on him the gift of continence. Let us consider, then, brethren, of what matter we were made—who and what manner of beings we came into the world, as it were out of a sepulchre, and from utter darkness. He who made us and fashioned us, having prepared His bountiful gifts for us before we were born, introduced us into His world. Since, therefore, we receive all these things from Him, we ought for everything to give Him thanks; to whom be glory for ever and ever. Amen.

Source: Alexander Roberts and James Donaldson, trans.; http://www.earlychristianwritings.com/text/1clement-roberts.html

The Myth of the Watchers

Before and during the first century c.e. a well-known legend circulated that expanded the story of Noah's flood. The basis of this story can be found in Genesis 6:1-4:

> [1] When people began to multiply on the face of the ground, and daughters were born to them, [2] the sons of God saw that they were fair; and they took wives for themselves of all that they chose.
>
> [3] Then the Lord said, "My spirit shall not abide in mortals forever, for they are flesh; their days shall be one hundred twenty years."
>
> [4] The Nephilim were on the earth in those days—and also afterward—when the sons of God went in to the daughters of humans, who bore children to them. These were the heroes that were of old, warriors of renown.

One of the several ancient texts that tells the story of the "Watchers" is in the book of Jubilees (written c. 100 b.c.e.). Two excerpts of this story are included here:

> And it came to pass when the children of men began to multiply on the face of the earth and daughters were born unto them, that the angels of God saw them on a certain year of this jubilee, that they were beautiful to look upon; and they took themselves wives of all whom they chose, and they bare unto them sons and they were giants. And lawlessness increased on the earth and all flesh corrupted its way, alike men and cattle and beasts and birds and everything that walks on the earth—all of them corrupted their ways and their orders, and they began to devour each other, and lawlessness increased on the earth and every imagination of the thoughts of all men (was) thus

evil continually. And God looked upon the earth, and behold it was corrupt, and all flesh had corrupted its orders, and all that were upon the earth had wrought all manner of evil before His eyes. And He said that He would destroy man and all flesh upon the face of the earth which He had created. But Noah found grace before the eyes of the Lord. And against the angels whom He had sent upon the earth, He was exceedingly wroth, and He gave commandment to root them out of all their dominion, and He bade us to bind them in the depths of the earth, and behold they are bound in the midst of them, and are (kept) separate. (Jubilees 5:1-6)

Source: R. H. Charles, trans.; http://www.pseudepigrapha.com/jubilees/index.htm

[Noah prayed before the Lord his God, and said:] "And Thou knowest how Thy Watchers, the fathers of these spirits, acted in my day: and as for these spirits which are living, imprison them and hold them fast in the place of condemnation, and let them not bring destruction on the sons of thy servant, my God; for these are malignant, and created in order to destroy. And let them not rule over the spirits of the living; for Thou alone canst exercise dominion over them. And let them not have power over the sons of the righteous from henceforth and for evermore." And the Lord our God bade us to bind all. And the chief of the spirits, Mastêmâ, came and said: "Lord, Creator, let some of them remain before me, and let them harken to my voice, and do all that I shall say unto them; for if some of them are not left to me, I shall not be able to

execute the power of my will on the sons of men; for these are for corruption and leading astray before my judgment, for great is the wickedness of the sons of men." And He said: "Let the tenth part of them remain before him, and let nine parts descend into the place of condemnation." And one of us He commanded that we should teach Noah all their medicines; for He knew that they would not walk in uprightness, nor strive in righteousness. And we did according to all His words: all the malignant evil ones we bound in the place of condemnation and a tenth part of them we left that they might be subject before Satan on the earth. And we explained to Noah all the medicines of their diseases, together with their seductions, how he might heal them with herbs of the earth. And Noah wrote down all things in a book as we instructed him concerning every kind of medicine. Thus the evil spirits were precluded from (hurting) the sons of Noah. (Jubilees 10:5-13)

Source: R. H. Charles, trans.; http://www.pseudepigrapha.com/jubilees/index.htm

Having read portions of the "Myth of the Watchers" from the book of Jubilees, take a look at the following New Testament texts:

[18] For Christ also suffered for sins once for all, the righteous for the unrighteous, in order to bring you to God. He was put to death in the flesh, but made alive in the spirit, [19] in which also he went and made a proclamation to the spirits in prison . . . (1 Peter 3:18-19)

⁴ For certain intruders have stolen in among you, people who long ago were designated for this condemnation as ungodly, who pervert the grace of our God into licentiousness and deny our only Master and Lord, Jesus Christ. ⁵ Now I desire to remind you, though you are fully informed, that the Lord, who once for all saved a people out of the land of Egypt, afterward destroyed those who did not believe. ⁶ And the angels who did not keep their own position, but left their proper dwelling, he has kept in eternal chains in deepest darkness for the judgment of the great Day. ⁷ Likewise, Sodom and Gomorrah and the surrounding cities, which, in the same manner as they, indulged in sexual immorality and pursued unnatural lust, serve as an example by undergoing a punishment of eternal fire. (Jude 1:4-7)

⁷ For a man ought not to have his head veiled, since he is the image and reflection of God; but woman is the reflection of man. ⁸ Indeed, man was not made from woman, but woman from man. ⁹ Neither was man created for the sake of woman, but woman for the sake of man. ¹⁰ For this reason a woman ought to have a symbol of authority on her head, because of the angels. ¹¹ Nevertheless, in the Lord woman is not independent of man or man independent of woman. ¹² For just as woman came from man, so man comes through woman; but all things come from God. (1 Corinthians 11:7-12)

Who are the "the spirits in prison"? Who are the "angels who did not keep their own position"? Why must women not tempt the angels?

Questions for Group Discussion

1. What is the purpose of imagining Jesus as a High Priest in Early Christianity?
2. What points of similarity are there between 1 Clement and the letters in the New Testament?
3. Who is Mastêmâ?

Questions for Reflection

1. How might the ideology of Hebrews have contributed to anti-Jewish doctrines in Christian tradition?

2. Does the Myth of the Watchers help to explain any of the New Testament passages listed above?

17

Revelation: John's Apocalyptic Vision

Summary and Learning Objectives

1. Revelation (often referred to *incorrectly* in the plural: "Revelations") is a series of letters followed by a series of visions. While there is a longstanding desire among Christians to use John's symbols as mirrors for contemporary politics, John is much more interested in the politics of his own day. After reading this chapter (alongside chapter 17 of Sumney's text), the reader should be able *to interpret a handful of symbols featured in Revelation.*

2. After reading this chapter (alongside chapter 17 of Sumney's text), the reader should be able *to offer at least three different interpretations of the phrase "Son of Man."*

3. After reading this chapter (alongside chapter 17 of Sumney's text), the reader should be able *to identify commonalities between Revelation and other forms of Jewish visionary texts.*

4. After reading this chapter (alongside chapter 17 of Sumney's text), the reader should be able *to speak to the difference between violent symbols and the nonviolent hopes they represent.*

Key Terms

Apocalypse, apocalyptic A genre of literature (apocalypse) and a way of understanding the world (apocalyptic). In this genre, a heavenly being brings a message about God's actions to enact justice. Both the literature and the world-view envision this action happening soon. The fullest example of the genre in the New Testament is the book of Revelation.

Eschatology Study of the end times, when it will be, and what is to happen at that time. Often this area of study also includes discussion of the state of the dead in the present.

Patmos Island off the western coast of Turkey where John had been exiled when he wrote Revelation.

Persecution Unjust opposition experienced because of one's beliefs or identity.

Son of Man Could be translated "son of a human." This ambiguous phrase could refer simply to a person or a mortal, but in the Gospels it designates Jesus as one who has an eschatological role. When these writers provide any clues about the phrase's meaning, it refers to the one who comes on the clouds bringing God's judgment. This understanding develops from the use of the expression in Daniel 7:13-14.

Key Themes

▶ Many symbols in Revelation can be clearly interpreted by understanding the literary conventions used by John

▶ Some violent metaphors convey nonviolent hopes

Primary Text

The Son of Man

The first apocalyptic vision of Revelation is of a Christ figure. Take a look at Revelation 1:9-20:

> [9] I, John, your brother who share with you in Jesus the persecution and the kingdom and the patient endurance, was on the island called Patmos because of the word of God and the testimony of Jesus. [10] I was in the spirit on the Lord's day, and I heard behind me a loud voice like a trumpet [11] saying, "Write in a book what you see

and send it to the seven churches, to Ephesus, to Smyrna, to Pergamum, to Thyatira, to Sardis, to Philadelphia, and to Laodicea." [12] Then I turned to see whose voice it was that spoke to me, and on turning I saw seven golden lampstands, [13] and in the midst of the lampstands I saw one like the Son of Man, clothed with a long robe and with a golden sash across his chest. [14] His head and his hair were white as white wool, white as snow; his eyes were like a flame of fire, [15] his feet were like burnished bronze, refined as in a furnace, and his voice was like the sound of many waters. [16] In his right hand he held seven stars, and from his mouth came a sharp, two-edged sword, and his face was like the sun shining with full force. [17] When I saw him, I fell at his feet as though dead. But he placed his right hand on me, saying, "Do not be afraid; I am the first and the last, [18] and the living one. I was dead, and see, I am alive forever and ever; and I have the keys of Death and of Hades. [19] Now write what you have seen, what is, and what is to take place after this. [20] As for the mystery of the seven stars that you saw in my right hand, and the seven golden lampstands: the seven stars are the angels of the seven churches, and the seven lampstands are the seven churches.

John, claiming to be writing from the island Patmos, sees seven golden lampstands that represent (so we are told) seven churches. Standing in the middle of these lampstands is "one like the Son of Man." This phrase evokes several meanings at once for John's readers. 1) It reminds us that Jesus called himself by the title "Son of Man." 2) It reminds us that apocalyptic visions often refer to human-looking figures (as opposed to animalized figures) by this title. 3) It reminds us that Daniel 7:13 refers to a figure by this title who may represent Israel collectively who has been elevated to an almost divine status. Read Daniel 7 carefully. Look closely for the interpretations offered by Daniel's guide:

> [1] In the first year of King Belshazzar of Babylon, Daniel had a dream and visions of his head as he lay in bed. Then he wrote down the dream: [2] I, Daniel, saw in my vision by night the four winds of heaven stirring up the great sea, [3] and four great beasts came up out of the sea, different from one another. [4] The first was like a lion and had eagles' wings. Then, as I watched, its wings were plucked off, and it was lifted up from the ground and made to stand on two feet like a human being; and a human mind was given to it. [5] Another beast appeared, a second one, that looked like a bear. It was raised up on one side, had three tusks in its mouth among its teeth and was told, "Arise, devour many bodies!" [6] After this, as I watched, another appeared, like a leopard. The beast had four wings of a bird on its back and four heads; and dominion was given to it. [7] After this I saw in the visions by night a fourth beast, terrifying and dreadful and exceedingly strong. It had great iron teeth and was devouring, breaking in pieces, and stamping what was left with its feet. It was different from all the beasts that preceded it, and it had ten horns. [8] I was considering the horns, when another horn appeared, a little one coming up among them; to make room for it, three of the earlier horns were plucked up by the roots. There were eyes like human eyes in this horn, and a mouth speaking arrogantly.

> [9] As I watched,
> thrones were set in place,
>> and an Ancient One took his throne,
> his clothing was white as snow,
>> and the hair of his head like pure wool;
> his throne was fiery flames,
>> and its wheels were burning fire.
> [10] A stream of fire issued
>> and flowed out from his presence.
> A thousand thousands served him,
>> and ten thousand times ten thousand
>>> stood attending him.
> The court sat in judgment,
>> and the books were opened.

> [11] I watched then because of the noise of the arrogant words that the horn was speaking. And as I watched, the beast was put to death, and its body destroyed and given over to be burned with fire. [12] As for the rest of the beasts, their dominion was taken away, but their lives were prolonged for a season and a time. [13] As I watched in the night visions,

> I saw one like a human being
>> coming with the clouds of heaven.
> And he came to the Ancient One
>> and was presented before him.
> [14] To him was given dominion
>> and glory and kingship,
> that all peoples, nations, and languages
>> should serve him.
> His dominion is an everlasting dominion
>> that shall not pass away,
> and his kingship is one
>> that shall never be destroyed.

[15] As for me, Daniel, my spirit was troubled within me, and the visions of my head terrified me. [16] I approached one of the attendants to ask him the truth concerning all this. So he said that he would disclose to me the interpretation of the matter: [17] "As for these four great beasts, four kings shall arise out of the earth. [18] But the holy ones of the Most High shall receive the kingdom and possess the kingdom forever—forever and ever." [19] Then I desired to know the truth concerning the fourth beast, which was different from all the rest, exceedingly terrifying, with its teeth of iron and claws of bronze, and which devoured and broke in pieces, and stamped what was left with its feet; [20] and concerning the ten horns that were on its head, and concerning the other horn, which came up and to make room for which three of them fell out—the horn that had eyes and a mouth that spoke arrogantly, and that seemed greater than the others. [21] As I looked, this horn made war with the holy ones and was prevailing over them, [22] until the Ancient One came; then judgment was given for the holy ones of the Most High, and the time arrived when the holy ones gained possession of the kingdom. [23] This is what he said: "As for the fourth beast, there shall be a fourth kingdom on earth that shall be different from all the other kingdoms; it shall devour the whole earth, and trample it down, and break it to pieces. [24] As for the ten horns, out of this kingdom ten kings shall arise, and another shall arise after them. This one shall be different from the former ones, and shall put down three kings. [25] He shall speak words against the Most High, shall wear out the holy ones of the Most High, and shall attempt to change the sacred seasons and the law; and they shall be given into his power for a time, two times, and half a time. [26] Then the court shall sit in judgment, and his dominion shall be taken away, to be consumed and totally destroyed. [27] The kingship and dominion and the greatness of the kingdoms under the whole heaven shall be given to the people of the holy ones of the Most High; their kingdom shall be an everlasting kingdom, and all dominions shall serve and obey them." [28] Here the account ends. As for me, Daniel, my thoughts greatly terrified me, and my face turned pale; but I kept the matter in my mind. (Daniel 7:1-28)

Notice that in Daniel 7:14 the "Son of Man" (translated as "a human being" above) is given "an everlasting dominion that shall not pass away." We are then told in 7:18 that "the holy ones of the Most High shall receive the kingdom and possess the kingdom forever—forever and ever." This may suggest that the singular figure the Son of Man represents a group called "the holy ones of the Most High." In this case, the human-looking figure may represent Israel, while the bestial figures represent other passing empires. Revelation, like much of apocalyptic literature, does this often: a singular figure represents an entire people. Another example of this is the title "The Bride" which clearly refers to the collective identity of the church.

War Poured Out from Heaven

The book of Revelation is rife with warfare. This metaphorical violence is meant to comfort a people who believe that they suffer persecution. Their hope is that God (in Christ) will return to administer justice. Such visions of war and judgment were not uncommon during this period. Consider 1 Enoch 102:1-11, a text written in a Jewish context before the emergence of early Christianity:

> In those days, when He shall cast the calamity of fire upon you, whither will you fly, and where will you be safe? And when He sends forth his word against you, are you not spared, and terrified? All the luminaries are agitated with great fear; and all the earth is spared, while it trembles, and suffers anxiety. All the angels fulfill the commands received by them, and are desirous of being concealed from the presence of the great Glory; while the children of the earth are alarmed and troubled. But you, sinners, are for ever accursed; to you there shall be no peace. Fear not, souls of the righteous; but wait with patient hope for the day of your death in righteousness. Grieve not, because your souls descend in great trouble, with groaning, lamentation, and sorrow, to the receptacle of the dead. In your lifetime your bodies have not received a recompense in proportion to your goodness, but in the period of your existence have sinners existed; in the period of execration and of punishment. And when you die, sinners say concerning you, As we die, the righteous die. What profit have they in their works? Behold, like us, they expire in sorrow and in darkness. What advantage have they over us? Henceforward are we equal. What will be within their grasp, and what before their eyes for ever? For behold they are dead; and never will they again perceive the light. I say unto you,

sinners, You have been satisfied with meat and drink, with human plunder and rapine, with sin, with the acquisition of wealth and with the sight of good days. Have you not marked the righteous, how their end is in peace? For no oppression is found in them even to the day of their death. They perish, and are as if they were not, while their souls descend in trouble to the receptacle of the dead.

Source: Richard Laurence, trans.; http://www.earlyjewishwritings.com/1enoch.html

Oral Weaponry

In Isaiah 11:3-4 we read of a wise king who can bring justice to the land simply by the power of his tongue. Isaiah 11:3-4 reads:

> [3] His delight shall be in the fear of the Lord. He shall not judge by what his eyes see, or decide by what his ears hear; [4] but with righteousness he shall judge the poor, and decide with equity for the meek of the earth; he shall strike the earth with the rod of his mouth, and with the breath of his lips he shall kill the wicked.

In this vision the poor and meek are cared for while the wicked are destroyed. But it is crucial to note that this leader does not conquer them with a literal weapon, but with "the rod of his mouth." This is a metaphor for potent and effective words of judgment that bring peace rather than war. In other words, this ruler (called the "prince of peace" in Isaiah 9:6) brings righteousness and justice by his powerful speech. As similar ruler (perhaps a messianic figure) is described in 2 Esdras (also called 4 Ezra) 13:8-13:

⁸ After this I looked, and behold, all who had gathered together against him [the "man"], to wage war with him, were much afraid, yet dared to fight. ⁹ And behold, when he saw the onrush of the approaching multitude, he neither lifted his hand nor held a spear or any weapon of war; ¹⁰ but I saw only how he sent forth from his mouth as it were a stream of fire, and from his lips a flaming breath, and from his tongue he shot forth a storm of sparks. ¹¹ All these were mingled together, the stream of fire and the flaming breath and the great storm, and fell on the onrushing multitude which was prepared to fight, and burned them all up, so that suddenly nothing was seen of the innumerable multitude but only the dust of ashes and the smell of smoke. When I saw it, I was amazed. ¹² After this I saw the same man come down from the mountain and call to him another multitude which was peaceable. ¹³ Then many people came to him, some of whom were joyful and some sorrowful; some of them were bound, and some were bringing others as offerings.

In this vision, the figure clear refuses to use "any weapon of war." Rather, he breaths a "stream of fire." This imagery borrows from Isaiah 11:4 (as seen above) and is meant again to contrast the power of speech with literal warfare. With this in mind, take a look at Revelation 19:11-21:

> ¹¹ Then I saw heaven opened, and there was a white horse! Its rider is called Faithful and True, and in righteousness he judges and makes war. ¹² His eyes are like a flame of fire, and on his head are many diadems; and he has a name inscribed that no one knows but himself. ¹³ He is clothed in a robe dipped in blood, and his name is called The Word of God. ¹⁴ And the armies of heaven, wearing fine linen, white and pure, were following him on white horses. ¹⁵ From his mouth comes a sharp sword with which to strike down the nations, and he will rule them with a rod of iron; he will tread the wine press of the fury of the wrath of God the Almighty. ¹⁶ On his robe and on his thigh he has a name inscribed, "King of kings and Lord of lords."
>
> ¹⁷ Then I saw an angel standing in the sun, and with a loud voice he called to all the birds that fly in mid-heaven, "Come, gather for the great supper of God, ¹⁸ to eat the flesh of kings, the flesh of captains, the flesh of the mighty, the flesh of horses and their riders—flesh of all, both free and slave, both small and great." ¹⁹ Then I saw the beast and the kings of the earth with their armies gathered to make war against the rider on the horse and against his army. ²⁰ And the beast was captured, and with it the false prophet who had performed in its presence the signs by which he deceived those who had received the mark of the beast and those who worshipped its image. These two were thrown alive into the lake of fire that burns with sulphur. ²¹ And the rest were killed by the sword of the rider on the horse, the sword that came from his mouth; and all the birds were gorged with their flesh.

Given that the sword comes from the mouth of Christ in this passage—not held in his hand—what does this suggest about Christ? Does this passage suggest literal warfare, or the power of speech?

Questions for Group Discussion

1. What does the phrase "Son of Man" mean in Daniel? What does it mean in Revelation?
2. What does the image of a sword for a tongue symbolize?
3. In what contexts is "judgment" comforting? In what contexts is "judgment" discomforting?

Questions for Reflection

1. In what ways can a violent text like Revelation bring hope to an oppressed people?

2. Read Revelation 21–22. How many people "go to heaven" in this final vision?

3. What is the final hope conveyed by John?

A SHORT GUIDE TO WRITING EXEGETICAL RESEARCH PAPERS

This guide is meant to help you organize and compose an exegetical research paper. You may also find portions of this sequence and resources helpful in other disciplines.

Short or long, your exegetical paper can be crafted in six steps: 1) choose a text or topic, 2) study the text yourself, 3) study the secondary literature, 4) outline your argument, 5) write the first draft, and 6) refine the final paper.

1. Choose a Text or Topic

If your text or topic is not chosen for you, you should aim to choose one that is 1) interesting to you, 2) manageable (with readily available sources) and malleable (so you can narrow in on an especially interesting or important aspect), and 3) arguable. Your exegetical research paper will essentially be an analysis of a particular passage of text, forming an *argument* based on this analysis along with the available secondary sources and authorities.

A good place to start is the chapters of *The Bible: An Introduction*. Perhaps there was a text or theme in one of the chapters (such as passages from the book of Judges and what they say about role of women in the ancient world) that caught your interest. Also, look over this study guide. Did one of the additional readings intrigue you?

2. Study the Text Yourself

Begin by reading through your chosen passage to develop your first impressions, noting any questions that arise for you as you read. Various methods of biblical exegesis can be helpful for you as you analyze the text, including:

Composition History

Is there a named author of the text? What do we know about him, her, or them? Is the attributed author the actual author, or is the work pseudepigraphic? When, where, and under what circumstances was the text written? Who seem to be the text's recipients?

Redaction Criticism

How has the author used the source or sources in shaping this text? Are there any parallel texts and how is this text similar or different? What particular views or theological emphases does the author show? How did the authors life circumstances (if they are known) affect the shaping of the text?

Literary Criticism

What words are used, and what range of meanings do they have? If you are able to read and analyze the text in its original language, do so! This will enrich your analysis. What images and symbols are used? What characters appear in the story? What are we told and what can you surmise about these characters? How are the characters related to one another in the story?

Comparison of Translations

Consider reading several English translations of the text. Are there any significant differences between translations? Which ancient Hebrew or Greek texts underlie the various translations? Does anything seem to have been lost or added in the process of translation?

Source Criticism

Does the text have any underlying source or sources? Does it quote from elsewhere in scripture? Which version of a source was used, in case there is more than one? What do the sources actually say and mean in their original contexts? How are the sources used (quoted, paraphrased, adapted?) in your text?

RELATED BIBLICAL OR ANCIENT TEXTS

In addition to looking for the quotation of other biblical texts, you may detect some thematic similarity between your chosen text and other passages in the Bible. Does your text seem to be an allusion to another text? What passages surround your text? From where has the reader just come, and where will the reader go next?

Form Criticism

What is the literary form or genre of the text? Does the text follow or diverge from the typical expectations and style of this genre? What is the customary purpose or goal of this genre? In what social context would texts of this genre been used?

Socio-Historical Criticism

What social, historical, or cultural information can be gleaned from the text? What background information is necessary to better understand the text? What was life like for people living in this time? If the story claims to be historical, what really happened?

History of Interpretation

How has this text been interpreted over time? What are the most common questions raised and theses posed about this text? Has opinion or interpretation changed? What events or discoveries led to such change?

Of course, these comprise just some of the many available strategies for interpreting biblical material. You'll likely draw from several strategies as you work toward your own conclusions. Placing your interpretation in conversation with the work of other scholars will help clarify and strengthen your thinking.

3. Study the Secondary Literature

Material about your text or topic may reside in a single resource or an array of works by one or many authors or in the conflicting opinions of contemporary scholars. In most cases, you can build your research by moving from general to specific treatments of your text.

One caution: In your research, take care not to allow your expanding knowledge of what others think about your text or topic to drown your own curiosities, sensibilities, and insights. Instead, as your initial questions expand and then diminish with increased knowledge from your research, your own deeper concerns, insights, and point of view should emerge and grow.

Encyclopedia articles, scholarly books, commentaries, journal articles, and other standard reference tools contain a wealth of material and helpful bibliographies to orient you to your text and its interpretation. Look for the most authoritative and up-to-date sources. Checking cross-references will deepen your knowledge.

It's wise to start listing the sources you've consulted right away in standard citation or footnote format (see section 6, below, for examples of usual formats). You'll want to assign a number or code to each one so you'll be able to reference them easily when you're writing the paper.

Reference Resources

Concordances

R. E. Whitaker and J. R. Kohlenberger III, *The Analytical Concordance to the New Revised Standard Version of the Bible* (Oxford: Oxford University Press, 2000)

Bible Dictionaries

W. R. F. Browning, ed., *A Dictionary of the Bible,* 2nd ed. (Oxford: Oxford University Press, 2009)

M. A. Powell, ed., *HarperCollins Bible Dictionary,* rev. and updated (San Francisco: HarperOne, 2011)

D. N. Freedman, ed., *The Anchor Bible Dictionary,* 6 vols. (New York: Doubleday, 1992)

Katharine Doob Sakenfeld, ed., *New Interpreter's Dictionary of the Bible* (Nashville: Abingdon Press, 2006)

COMMENTARIES

One- and two-volume:

J. L. Mays, *The HarperCollins Bible Commentary*, rev. ed. (San Francisco: HarperOne, 2000)

R. E. Brown, J. A. Fitzmyer, and R. E. Murphy, eds., *The New Jerome Biblical Commentary*, 3rd ed. (Upper Saddle River, NJ: Prentice Hall, 1999)

J. Barton and J. Muddiman, eds., *The Oxford Bible Commentary* (Oxford: Oxford University Press, 2001)

G. A. Yee, H. R. Page Jr., and M. J. M. Coomber, eds., *Fortress Commentary on the Bible: The Old Testament and Apocrypha* (Minneapolis: Fortress Press, 2014)

M. Aymer, C. B. Kittredge, and D. A. Sánchez, eds., *Fortress Commentary on the Bible: The New Testament* (Minneapolis: Fortress Press, 2014)

Online Resources

A list of resources for research in biblical studies is available at the homepage of the Society of Biblical Literature, here: http://www.sbl-site.org/educational/researchtools.aspx

Periodical Literature

Even though your own interpretation should drive your exegesis, you'll be able to place your interpretation in contemporary context only by referring to what other scholars today are saying. Their work is largely published in academic journals and periodicals. In consulting the chief articles dealing with your topic, you'll learn where agreements, disagreements, and open questions stand; how older treatments have fared; and the latest relevant tools and insights. Since you cannot consult them all, work back from the latest, looking for the best and most directly relevant articles from the last five, ten, or twenty years, as ambition and time allow.

A good place to start is the ATLA Religion Database (http://www.atla.com), which indexes articles, essays, book reviews, dissertations, theses, and even essays in collections. You can search by keywords, subjects, persons, or scripture references. Below are other standard indexes to periodical literature. Check with your institution's library to learn which ones it subscribes to.

Guide to Social Science and Religion in Periodical Literature (http://www.nplguide.com)
Readers' Guide to Periodical Literature
Dissertation Abstracts International
ATLA Catholic Periodical and Literature Index
Humanities International Index

Identify the Most Important Secondary Sources

By now you can identify the most important sources for your text or topic, both primary and secondary. Apart from books and journal articles you've identified, you can find the chief works on any topic readily listed in your college or seminary library's catalog, the Library of Congress subject index (http://catalog2.loc.gov), and other online library catalog sites. Many theological libraries and archives are linked at the "Religious Studies Web Guide": http://www.ucalgary.ca/~lipton/catalogues.html

The eventual quality of your exegetical paper rests soundly (though not exclusively) on the quality or critical character of your sources. The best research uses academically sound treatments by recognized authorities arguing rigorously from primary sources.

Take Notes

Now review each source, noting down its most important or relevant facts, observations, or opinions. Be sure to keep your notes organized consistently; you may choose to create a separate document for the notes on each source you consult, for example. As you take notes, you should identify the subtopic, the source information (including page numbers), and the main idea or direct quotation.

While most of the notes you take will simply summarize points made in primary or secondary sources, direct quotes are used for 1) word-for-word transcriptions, 2) key words or phrases coined by the author, or 3) especially clear or summary formulations of an author's point of view. Remember, re-presenting another's insight or formulation without attribution is plagiarism. You should also be sure to keep separate notes about your own ideas or insights into the text or topic as they evolve.

When Can I Stop?

As you research your text in books, articles, or reference works, you will find it coalescing into a unified body of knowledge or at least into a set of interrelated questions. Your topic will become more and more focused, partly because that is where the open question or key insight or most illuminating instance resides and partly for sheer manageability. The vast range of scholarly methods, opinions, and sharply differing points of view about most biblical texts (especially in the contemporary period) may force you to narrow your topic further. While the sources may never dry up, your increased knowledge will gradually give you confidence that you have the most informed, authoritative, and critical sources covered in your notes.

4. Outline Your Argument

On the basis of your research findings and your own interpretation of the text, in this crucial step you refine or reformulate your general interpretation into a specific question about the text answered by a defensible thesis. You then arrange or rework your supporting materials into a clear outline that will coherently and convincingly present your thesis to your reader.

First, review your research notes carefully. Some of what you initially read may now seem obvious or irrelevant, or perhaps the whole topic is simply too massive. As your reading and note taking progressed, however, you might also have found a piece of your topic, from which a key question or problem has emerged and around which your research has gelled. Ask yourself:

▶ What is the subtopic or subquestion presented by this text that is most interesting, enlightening, and manageable?
▶ Which other biblical or ancient texts surround this text, are related to it, or raise similar questions?
▶ What have been the most clarifying and illuminating insights I have found in my research?

▶ In what ways have my findings contradicted my initial expectations? Can this serve as a clue to a new and different approach to the text?

▶ Can I frame a question about this text in a clear way, and, in light of my research, do I have something new to say and defend—my thesis—that will answer my question and clarify my materials?

In this way, you will advance from general interpretation to specific question and thesis. For example, as you research primary and secondary sources on the role of women in the book of Judges, you might find that women are portrayed in this biblical text as tricksters who use creative means to achieve their goals, even while marginalized. You might then advance a thesis that biblical heroines such as Deborah were able to subvert their typically marginalized role in society and achieve their desired ends through innovative and even revolutionary means. So you have: *Example:*

Topic:	Women in the book of Judges
Specific topic:	Women as tricksters in the book of Judges
Specific question:	How did Deborah achieve her goals as a marginalized person in a patriarchal society?
Thesis:	Deborah serves as one example of the trickster type in the Bible, displaying the subversive potential of biblical women to achieve their goals.

You can then outline a presentation of your thesis that organizes your research materials into an orderly and convincing argument. Functionally your outline might look like this:

Introduction:	Raise the key question and announce your thesis.
Background:	Summarize your text and present the necessary textual or historical or theological context of the question. Note the "state of the question" or the main agreements and disagreements about it.
Development:	Present your own insight in a clear and logical way. Present evidence to support your thesis, and develop it further by:

▶ offering examples from the text itself

▶ Pointing to related biblical or ancient texts

▶ citing or discussing authorities to bolster your argument

▶ contrasting your thesis with other treatments, either historical or contemporary

▶ confirming it by showing how it makes good sense of the text, answers related questions, or solves previous puzzles.

Conclusion:	Restate the thesis in a way that recapitulates your argument and its consequences for the field or the contemporary religious horizon.

The more detailed your outline, the easier your writing will be. Go through your notes, reorganizing them according to your outline. Fill in the outline with the specifics from your research, right down to the topic sentences of your paragraphs. Don't hesitate to set aside any materials that now seem off-point, extraneous, or superfluous to the development of your argument.

5. Write the First Draft

You are now ready to draft your paper, essentially by putting your outline into sentence form while incorporating specifics from your research notes.

Your main task, initially, is just to set your ideas down in as straightforward a way as possible. Assume your reader is intelligent but knows little or nothing about your particular topic or the text being discussed. You can follow your outline closely, but you may find that logical presentation of your argument requires making some adjustments to the outline. As you write, weave in quotes judiciously from primary and secondary literature to clarify or punch your points. Add brief, strong headings at major junctures. Add footnotes to acknowledge ideas, attribute quotations, reinforce your key points through authorities, or refer the reader to further discussion or resources. Your draft footnotes will refer to your sources as abbreviated in your notes, and be sure to include page numbers. You can add full publishing data once your text is firm.

6. Refine the Final Paper

Your first draft puts you within sight of your goal, but your project's real strength emerges from reworking your initial text in a series of revisions and refinements.

In this final phase, make frequent use of one of the many excellent style manuals available for help with grammar, punctuation, footnote form, abbreviations, and so forth:

▶ Alexander, Patrick H., et al., eds. *The SBL Handbook of Style: For Ancient Near Eastern, Biblical, and Early Christian Studies*. Peabody, Mass.: Hendrickson, 1999.
▶ *The Chicago Manual of Style*. 15th ed. Chicago: University of Chicago Press, 2003.
▶ Turabian, Kate L. *A Manual for Writers of Term Papers, Theses, and Dissertations*. 7th ed. Rev. by Wayne C. Booth, Gregory G. Colomb, Joseph M. Williams, and the University of Chicago Press Editorial Staff. Chicago: University of Chicago Press, 2007.

Online, see the searchable website Guide to Grammar and Writing: http://grammar.ccc.commnet.edu/grammar/

Polishing the Prose

To check spelling and meaning of words or to help vary your prose, try Merriam-Webster Online, which contains both the Collegiate Dictionary and the Thesaurus: http://www.m-w.com.

Closely examine your work several times, paying attention to:

▶ Structure and Argument. Ask yourself, do I state my question and thesis accurately? Does my paper do what my introduction promised? (If not, adjust one or the other.) Do I argue my thesis well? Do the headings clearly guide the reader through my outline and argument? Does this sequence of topics orchestrate the insights my reader needs to understand my thesis?

▶ Style. "Style" here refers to writing patterns that enliven prose and engage the reader. Three simple ways to strengthen your academic prose are:

—Topic sentences: Be sure each paragraph clearly states its main assertion.

—Active verbs: As much as possible, avoid using the linking verb "to be," and instead rephrase using active verbs.

—Sentence flow: Above all, look for awkward sentences in your draft. Disentangle and rework them into smooth, clear sequences. To avoid boring the reader, vary the length and form of your sentences. Check to see if your paragraphs unfold with questions and simple declarative sentences, in addition to longer descriptive phrases.

Likewise, tackle some barbarisms that frequently invade academic prose:

—Repetition: Unless you need the word count, this can go.

—Unnecessary words: Such filler phrases as "The fact that" and "in order to" and "There is" or "There are" numb your reader. Similarly, such qualifiers as "somewhat," "fairly," and "very" should be avoided unless they are part of a clearly defined comparison.

—Jargon. Avoid technical terms when possible. Explain all technical terms that you do use. Avoid or translate foreign-language terms.

—Overly complex sentences. Short sentences are best. Beware of run-on sentences. Avoid "etc."

Along with typographical errors, look for stealth errors—the common but overlooked grammatical gaffes: subject-verb disagreement, dangling participles, mixed verb tenses, overuse and underuse of commas, misuse of semicolons, and inconsistency in capitalization, hyphenation, italicization, and treatment of numbers.

Footnotes

Your footnotes credit your sources for every direct quotation and for other people's ideas you have used. Below are samples of typical citation formats following *The Chicago Manual of Style*. (For a basic summary of *The Chicago Manual of Style*, visit http://www.chicagomanualofstyle.org/tools_citationguide.html)

▶ Basic order
Author's full name, *Book Title,* ed., trans., series, edition, vol. number (Place: Publisher, year), pages.

▶ Book
Amy Kalmanofsky, *Dangerous Sisters of the Hebrew Bible* (Minneapolis: Fortress Press, 2014), 101–118.

▶ Book in a series
Marcus J. Borg, *Conflict, Holiness, and Politics in the Teaching of Jesus*, Studies in the Bible and Early Christianity 5 (Toronto: Edwin Mellen, 1984), 1–2.

▶ Essay or chapter in an edited book
Yak-Hwee Tan, "The Johannine Community," in *Soundings in Cultural Criticism*, ed. Francisco Lozada Jr. and Greg Carey (Minneapolis: Fortress Press, 2013), 84–85.

▶ Multivolume work

Karl Rahner, "On the Theology of Hope," *Theological Investigations*, vol. 10 (New York: Herder and Herder, 1973), 250.

▶ Journal article

Joan B. Burton, "Women's Commensality in the Ancient Greek World," *Greece and Rome* 45, no. 2 (October 1998): 144.

▶ Encyclopedia article

Hans-Josef Klauck, "Lord's Supper," in *The Anchor Bible Dictionary,* ed. David Noel Freedman, vol. 2 (New York: Doubleday, 1992), 275.

▶ Online journal article

Pamela Sue Anderson, "The Case for a Feminist Philosophy of Religion: Transforming Philosophy's Imagery and Myths," *Ars Disputandi* 1 (2000/2001); http://www.arsdisputandi.org.

▶ Citing the Bible

Cite in your text (not in your footnotes) by book, chapter, and verse: Gen. 1:1-2; Exod. 7:13; Rom. 5:1-8. In your Bibliography list the version of the Bible you have used.

If a footnote cites the immediately preceding source, use "Ibid." (from the Latin *ibidem*, meaning "there"). For example: 61. Ibid., 39.

Sources cited earlier can be referred to by author or editor's last name or names, a shorter title, and page number. For example: Burton, "Women's Commensality," 145.

Bibliography

Your bibliography can be any of several types:

▶ Works Cited: just the works—books, articles, etc.—that appear in your footnotes;

▶ Works Consulted: all the works you checked in your research, whether they were cited or not in the final draft; or

▶ Select Bibliography: primary and secondary works that, in your judgment, are the most important source materials on this topic, whether cited or not in your footnotes.

Some teachers might ask for your bibliographic entries to be annotated, that is, with a comment from you on the content, import, approach, and helpfulness of each work.

Bibliographic style differs somewhat from footnote style. Here are samples of typical bibliographic formats following *The Chicago Manual of Style*:

▶ Basic order

Author's last name, first name and initial. *Book Title.* Ed. Trans. Series. Edition. Vol. Place: Publisher, Year.

▶ Book

Kalmanofsky, Amy. *Dangerous Sisters of the Hebrew Bible.* Minneapolis: Fortress Press, 2014.

▶ Book in a series

Borg, Marcus J. *Conflict, Holiness, and Politics in the Teaching of Jesus.* Studies in the Bible and Early Christianity 5. Toronto: Edwin Mellen, 1984.

▶ Essay or chapter in an edited book

Tan, Yak-Hwee. "The Johannine Community." In *Soundings in Cultural Criticism*. Ed. Francisco Lozada Jr. and Greg Carey. Minneapolis: Fortress Press, 2013.

▶ Multivolume work

Rahner, Karl. "On the Theology of Hope." In *Theological Investigations*, vol. 10. New York: Herder and Herder, 1973.

▶ Journal article

Burton, Joan B. "Women's Commensality in the Ancient Greek World." *Greece and Rome* 45, no. 2 (October 1998): 143–65.

▶ Encyclopedia article

Klauck, Hans-Josef. "Lord's Supper." In *The Anchor Bible Dictionary*. Ed. David Noel Freedman. Vol. 2. New York: Doubleday, 1992.

▶ Online journal article

Anderson, Pamela Sue. "The Case for a Feminist Philosophy of Religion: Transforming Philosophy's Imagery and Myths." *Ars Disputandi* 1 (2000/2001); http://www.arsdisputandi.org.

▶ Citing the Bible

The Holy Bible: Revised Standard Version. New York: Oxford University Press, 1973.

Final Steps

After incorporating the revisions and refinements into your paper, print out a fresh copy, proofread it carefully, make your last corrections to the electronic file, format it to your teacher's or school's specifications, and print your final paper.